ART
OF
HOPE

ART OF HOPE

Emma Harot

iUniverse®

ART OF HOPE

iUniverse books may be ordered through booksellers or by contacting:

iUniverse
1663 Liberty Drive
Bloomington, IN 47403
www.iuniverse.com
1-800-Authors (1-800-288-4677)

ISBN: 978-1-5320-4102-0 (sc)
ISBN: 978-1-5320-4103-7 (e)

Library of Congress Control Number: 2018900310

Print information available on the last page.

iUniverse rev. date: 06/28/2018

THE DIAGNOSIS

"**M**Y EGGS ARE SCRAMBLED!" is the answer I've given a million times. That is, every time I'm asked why I adopted my children. People are so nosy. Complete strangers come up to me in the supermarket, take a look at me, then take a look at my kid and say, "He must look like your husband." People have a lot of nerve. What if I weren't married? And if my kids were adopted, why is this any of their business? I just continue picking out the best string beans in the produce aisle, hoping that everyone will leave me alone.

I never really wanted to write a book. True, my life has been quite an adventure for the last twenty-plus years, but who'd be interested in my story? Anyone can write a book today. How would my story be different, or more special, than any other memoir? I'm not famous. I definitely haven't done anything spectacular. I am a pretty average local Jane.

So why have I decided to finally tell my story?

My dear and precious reader, I wrote this book for you. You may be going through a lot right now, and I want to show you that you are not alone. This book describes how I survived many trials and tribulations in my life (otherwise known as: the junk that I had to endure).

So where do I begin? I guess from the beginning.

I had just turned twenty. I was working very hard at my studies in University, towards a degree in Occupational Therapy. It was one of those days that I wished I could just stay under the covers, in my cozy-fleece footed PJs that were covered in funky monkeys. It was the December holiday season and the whole world seemed to be jolly. Everywhere I went, I heard music and saw families shopping and spending time together.

I had no time for any of that. I was headed to my college campus via bus and two trains. I hated the commute yet I knew the only way I could help people through illness and other tragedies would be to go to a school that would train me to become the best therapist I could possibly be. I knew how much my own independence meant to me, and that without it, my quality of life would be severely diminished. So if someone had a stroke or an accident of some kind, I wanted to be the one to help him/her rehabilitate and become the person he/she was before. That is how I would make a difference in this world.

My favorite spot to study (or just get away from it all) was in the back-section of a little Starbucks, off of Route 109. I even had my own chair! It didn't have my name on it of course, but I knew that chair was mine, waiting patiently for me to come and visit. The café was always brimming with life. The aromas of freshly brewed coffee, cinnamon and pumpkin, always stir within me a yearning for a good, strong cup of coffee. I always ordered my coffee with a few generous squirts of sugar-free French vanilla flavoring. The pastries always looked amazing — until I'd note the white paper next to each one stating the exact number of calories in each! After mentally calculating exactly how long I'd have to work out the next day just to burn off the 8,000 calories in that two-inch donut, I'd end up walking away without it.

The cup of coffee always felt so warm in my hands. I would hold it close and take a big sniff. Pure ecstasy! Sometimes, the little things in life make us the happiest. I'd walk to "my" chair, plop my book bag down, and begin my regular study routine. My chair had two stains on the left armrest and a small hole on the right. It was a dinky, messed-up chair but mine nonetheless. It was where I went to study or just be. No one would bother me there. No one knew who I was. It was my happy place.

The year was 1992. I had my whole life ahead of me. I lived at home with my parents and brother Jacob, who was three years my junior. My brother and I were always there for each other and watched out for one another. My parents were amazing. I knew they would do anything for me and that gave me the self-confidence which got me through a lot in life. They were my soft cuddly blanket that I knew I could wrap myself in anytime I felt like it. That kind of love is worth a million bucks.

During the week we all went in our own directions. But weekends were sacred family time. We sat around our kitchen table, eating delicious food and talking. My father and I used to love to sing together during our long enjoyable family meals.

At the end of each song we sang, we would play a silly game of who could hold the last note the longest. It was our special game, like our own secret handshake. My father almost always won, but not by much! When I was around twenty, I began losing our little contest more and more frequently. I tried to hold the notes for as long as I could, but I could not stop coughing. First, I didn't think anything of it. Why should I? I was never sick a day in my life, aside from the normal viruses common in childhood. Finally, after this had gone on for quite some time, my father urged me to check it out. The following week, I saw a pulmonologist who concluded that I had a slight case of asthma. This, he said, was causing the shortness of breath and coughing. He instructed me to use an inhaler from then on. I remember telling my mother how upset I was to need this stupid inhaler. She told me that I was crazy, and that it was not a big deal. But to me, it was a huge deal. I'd never had any limitations nor had to take any medications before. This was something entirely new for me.

With the perspective of hindsight, how I wish that doctor's diagnosis had been correct! After a week of using the inhaler, we realized it just wasn't helping. My cough was getting worse with each passing week. I revisited that doctor to find out why the inhaler was not doing the trick. The doctor felt my neck, up and down. He got this inexplicably anxious look on his face. He advised me to go to the hospital to get a chest x-ray, just "to rule a few things out". I followed his advice immediately. At this time, I was not yet worried. I didn't know enough to be nervous. I was a healthy young woman. Why should I be nervous?

After I completed the x-ray, I watched nonchalantly as the doctors congregated by the x-ray light box, focused intently on my x-ray. What was there to discuss? My x-ray looked rather normal to me — except for this great, big smudge smack in the middle of it. Maybe the technician had been eating a slice of pizza at the time and gotten his oily, smudgy hands all over it? Some nerve!

I asked the doctor what was going on. He started telling me that this "could be a few different things" and that they could not be sure of a definitive diagnosis "until a biopsy was done". It was gibberish to me, as though he was talking in some other language. I told the doctor I didn't understand what any of this had to do with my asthma. I remember him having trouble getting the words out. He then uttered the words no one should ever have to hear.

"I am so sorry Emma, I think you might have cancer."

To say that his words shocked me is an understatement. I felt like I was watching a movie about someone else, in slow motion. The doctor was talking, but I couldn't hear a word he was saying. I watched how his mouth kept moving, but I heard nothing. It was as if my brain had shut off for a few minutes. Subconsciously, my body had put itself into a kind of coping/survival mode. Had it not, I would probably have had a heart attack, right on the spot.

My conscious mind panicked. This can't be happening. This is a joke, right? Where is the camera hidden? Will someone eventually pop out and tell me I've been had? But why would anyone be so cruel? Why would anyone do that to me? Maybe I was dreaming. I must be! I hoped it was just one of those nightmares you would swear was real, until you got up and realized that it was all a passing dream. I ordered myself to wake up. I pinched myself so hard, I think I drew blood. But no matter how hard I tried, I could not escape where I was. Then it hit me like a ton of bricks. This was really happening! Whether I liked it or not, and whether I was ready for it or not, this was my new reality. I had no choice in the matter. I had the **big scary 'C'** word. I was in absolute shock.

As the realization set in, my body began to shake uncontrollably. It started with my hands and then drifted downward until my whole body was trembling. I could barely speak, but I finally managed to ask the doctor if I could call my mother to pick me up. I told him I was scared and did not feel up to driving myself home. I still remember dialing the number thinking, what am I going to tell her? How do you call your mother one day at work and just blurt out news like this? All alone and more scared than I'd ever been in my entire life. I called my mother. She picked up and asked if everything was okay. I so wished I could tell her that everything was just fine.

"I think I have cancer!" I blurted out without warning. She began with the questions. That was when I started to cry. "I don't know anything!" I practically shouted at her. I asked her to please come down as soon as she could. As I waited, I thought: Is this my life? No, it couldn't be. My life was still intact. Soon I would be nervously awaiting my Thursday night date, and preparing to retake the math final I'd flunked the week before.

They put me in a room and told me to lie down on a cold, metal table. The technician kept telling me to breathe, and then hold my breath, to breathe and hold my breath. I remember trying to be extra nice to him. In denial mode, I really believed that if I was nice enough to the technician, he wouldn't give me any bad news. Well, I was super-duper nice to the guy, and he gave me terrible news anyway. So much for that theory!

The CT scan showed a large mass in the middle of my chest. Unsure of what the mass was, they suspected lymphoma. I remember having learned about the lymph node system in school. I never really understood it, or thought I would ever need to understand it. Within a period of two hours, I had gone from being a student whose worst problem was getting a C on my English paper to living out my worst fear.

Life is bizarre, because at approximately eight years of age,

I would tell people that my biggest fear in life was cancer. It had always been my biggest and deepest fear. At thirteen years old, spending a summer by the lake, all my friends baked in the sun, competing for the best tan. I was the only one yelling at my friends to "get out of the sun!" I would tell them that if they kept it up, they were going to look like a raisin one day, and that it was just plain unsafe. I had learned about skin cancer and stayed out of the sun like it was poison. At ten years old I was Miss Healthy, eating Fiber One cereal when all my friends were eating Apple Jacks and Cocoa Pebbles. I had read in some magazine that increasing your fiber intake lowered your chance of ever getting cancer. I never wanted to get this dreadful disease, so I did everything in my power to stay far away from whatever could cause it. I must have had some kind of psychic power. Ten years later, there I was, sitting in the hospital with my new diagnosis of Hodgkin's Lymphoma.

I came home and cried like I'd never cried before. I remember hearing my parents whispering in their bedroom later that night, with the door locked. I tried to put my ear to the door to hear what they were saying. Did they know something more that I didn't know? One thing I was sure of. My parents would never let anything bad happen to me. I just knew it. They would protect me. That was their job.

THE SCENT OF POISON

THE DOCTORS WASTED NO TIME. The next few days were filled with non-stop scans, chest x-rays, and biopsies of my lymph nodes. The following week, I received my first strong dose of chemotherapy in the hospital. I then spent the next week at home trying to recover, and get my blood counts back up to normal levels. The hardest part of this whole ordeal was that after feeling so sick in the hospital, I would return home and start to feel better-only to know that the next week the nightmare would begin all over again. The medications burned their way through my stomach lining, making me feel sick whenever I tried to eat.

They had meds to help with the nausea, but nothing gave me any relief. I was in a constant state of nausea due to "a cocktail" of chemotherapy drugs. The hospital actually calls it a cocktail. No, this is not some great alcoholic beverage! This cocktail, called ABVD, was a practically lethal mix of poisons that were being injected into my body.

The chemo is meant to kill the bad cancer cells. However, in the process it also kills good cells. My immune system was shot.

This is when I began to hate everything about hospitals. I couldn't stand the acrid smell of the poisonous medications. I hated the incessant beeping from the five hundred IV poles that were on my floor. Those IV machines beeped all day and night. It was maddening to me. I couldn't take it! Most of the time I was helpless to stop the noise, because I was the lowly patient hooked up to an IV pole. How could I reach a nurse to inform her about the beeping? Try using one of those Call Buttons to get a nurse to your room. What a joke! I mean, come on! A patient is literally captive! This pole has to go with you wherever you go because of the nonstop infusion of liquids, which makes you need the bathroom ten times a night. Try getting to that bathroom with your IV pole plugged into the wall! It always reaches almost up to the toilet but not quite. Once I decided to unplug the stupid machine, but the beeping just started all over again. I really believe that when people go to hell (or wherever the bad guys go) there will always be that incessant beeping, and that smell! The smell of antibacterial heavy-duty cleaners mixed with hospital-style chicken and peas. I would bet a million dollars that this is what goes on down there.

The nurses were not allowed to give me any kind of pain relief, even a basic Tylenol, without permission from my doctor. It was generally impossible to reach my doctor, and so, I would wait and wait all day for him to come in. Finally, it would be okay to give me my tiny pill. That is when I learned to bring my personal stash of "goodies" along with me to every hospital stay. Hospital regulations forbid any patient to have any of their own medications on the floor. But having a nervous breakdown (because the nurse can't give you anything to help with your insane pain) is legal. That the hospital allows. So I had to learn to beat the system. That meant my little black bag never left my side. Whenever a nurse or doctor entered my room, my little black bag would be out of sight. This was one way I learned to survive in this jungle. I used to say that even the healthiest person, given a week in the hospital, would become sick with something.

A hospital is not the place to get better. It is the place to get the meds you need, then run out of there as fast as your two feet can carry you.

Unfortunately, I know all too well about hospitals, since I spent many months in and out of the supposedly best ones. When I go into the hospital for whatever reason, my first and foremost question to my doctor is always the same. When can I get out of this hell on earth?

The ABVD made me very sick. I have never felt weakness like the weakness of chemotherapy and cancer. It is a feeling that only someone who has been down this road understands. It is a weakness that puts you into the most depressed and incapacitated state. Only a few weeks earlier, I was a strong, young woman who had all the energy in the world. I was just not used to any of this. I was used to doing everything on my own, and now I was a sick and sad patient who was losing power, even over my own body. This whole "sick thing" was just not for me!

After one week in the hospital, I couldn't wait to get out. By the time I arrived home, I was so weak, all I did was stay in bed day and night. I remember it was summertime, and as I looked out my small bedroom window. I could see my neighbors in the swimming pool having parties with all their friends. It wasn't anything fancy like those underground pools. It was a cheap, blue thing that was inflated at the beginning of each summer. They would always be laughing and having such a great time. I used to close my eyes and pretend that I was swimming with them, playing Marco Polo and not having a care in the world. I was so jealous that I would stare out that window for hours, watching them all live such normal lives. That used to be me. That used to be me playing Marco Polo, but not anymore. I would climb back into my bed and spend the rest of the afternoon drenching my pillow with tears of despair. I would think of how life was just so unfair. Every vestige of my former life was slowly being stripped away.

MY SECRET LIFE BEGINS

I HAD A VERY BIG decision to make at this time, and I still don't know if I did the right thing. However, I made my choice. I decided that when my diagnosis was confirmed, I would keep it a secret. No one was to know except my parents, my doctors, and myself. My oncologist agreed and said that after a few months it would all be over and I would look back at this phase in my life as a bad dream. He was the Doctor, so I believed him. I had thought long and hard about it, because going it alone would make the experience much more difficult. However, I was adamant that people outside my immediate family not be told. It had nothing to do with shame. I did not want the world to see me like this, because I loathed pity. I knew people would not treat me the same if they knew what was going on, no matter how hard they tried, and I was not ready to deal with that. People love to talk, and I refused to be the topic of discussion, and pity. I wanted to be treated like a regular young woman, no differently.

There was another very important reason why I felt I had to keep my diagnosis a secret. Two weeks before my diagnosis, I'd begun dating a guy by the name of Nathaniel whom I really liked, and that was rare for me. I liked him because he was sweet and gentle, and he made me laugh. He was the best storyteller I'd ever met, and I was never bored with him. But I had just met him and we'd only known each other for a few weeks. There was absolutely no reason for him to stand by me through this, and it couldn't be expected. However, I didn't want to lose him. I thought: This man might turn out to be the love of my life and I don't want to mess it up with this stupid cancer thing! Most new dates would have run for the hills upon hearing about an illness like this. I preferred to live one of my most painful years alone, rather than lose him.

The day my hair started falling out was probably one of the hardest days of my life. One night after my shower, I started brushing my long, beautiful curly hair. I loved my hair, as most girls do, and I used to spend hours brushing and styling it. It was in the early nineties, when we still believed that having our hair permed ten feet into the air actually made us look pretty. I mean, what were we thinking? As I began my twenty minute ritual of brushing and styling my long locks, I started seeing clumps of hair attached to my brush. The more I brushed, the more my hair came out. It didn't stop. I started to panic and began to brush my hair furiously, watching the bald spots appear all over my head. It all happened so fast. Pre-shower, I had a full head of hair, and post-shower I was as bald as a bowling ball, aside from my funny Fuzzies, as I use to call them. These Fuzzies looked like soft fur on top of my bald head. It wasn't bad enough that I was bald; I had to have Fuzzies to make me look even worse — if that was even possible. I don't know if I looked scary or just odd. I felt like a bizarre creature with sunken, sullen eyes and very pale skin.

The doctors told me that some people like to shave their hair before the chemo ravages it. I guess it gives them a sense of control. However, I did not delude myself into thinking that I had any say in anything that was happening to me at this stage of my life. I refused to make myself look sick in advance. Besides, I secretly hoped that I would be different and that somehow my hair, my beautiful hair, would be spared. What was happening to me? What was this thing doing to me? I couldn't take it. I looked in the mirror, and it was not me that I saw. It was some weird alien-like creature with a head that appeared two sizes too large for my body. I had lost so much weight, and I guess without hair, my bald head looked rather large and alarming. At one point, I just closed my eyes, fell to the floor, and proceeded to fall apart. I couldn't fool myself anymore and say, "Maybe this is not really happening." Now, every time I looked into the mirror, my own reflection would scream back to me, YOU HAVE CANCER! I hated my reflection, and I hated that I had cancer. I couldn't scream or even have a good cry. I was too weak for that. I just curled up into a ball on the bathroom floor and just began weeping like a baby.

I had to find a company that sold wigs. I needed to find something that would make me look like myself again, even if it was an illusion. I quickly learned that no matter how authentic the wig, or how many thousands of dollars you were willing to spend, it rarely looked exactly like your own hair. The wigs were ugly and made me look ten years older than I was. The cancer had also aged me about hundred years, so when I looked into the mirror with my new wig on, I looked old. Today wigs look great — not back then.

Before Nathaniel, I used to go out on many dates, but the thought of actually marrying one of them made me uneasy. I figured that whatever I'd read in books about romance was an illusion. Perhaps the whole idea of love was a complete fantasy. I didn't love Nathaniel yet, either. I did enjoy his company, though, and that was enough. I was firm in my decision to live this double life in order to keep him. Until this day, I have no idea how I did it. Nathaniel noticed that my hairstyle was different, but being a typical guy, he didn't think anything of it. Why would he? By nature, I am the kind of person that can't stand any kind of untruth. I was probably one of the most honest people that I knew, yet here I was, a decent human being, living a life of secrecy and deception. This whole charade was going against the very grain of my being. I had to keep reminding myself that this was a "wartime" of sorts. Sometimes in war, you have to do things to survive you would never otherwise do.

I remember feeling nauseous all the time. I couldn't even look at food. The doctors kept telling me, "You have to eat to keep up your strength." How could I eat when I felt like vomiting? Just not happening!

On the "off" weeks (no chemo) that I was home, I just wanted to stay in bed and recover. However, every Wednesday I had an appointment in the city to see the doctor and get my blood counts checked. Although my mother was working full-time throughout this whole ordeal, she had to take me to work on appointment days. She could not afford to lose her job. I had to get up at five in the morning, no matter how horrible I felt, get dressed, and head out with my mother to work. I stayed in her school building most of the day, until it was time for my mother to drive me into the city for my appointment. Those hours of being at her workplace felt like years to me. I would go up to an empty room in the building, find a spot on the floor to lay down and just wait until my mother came to get me. I remember going into one of those five-stall public bathrooms and gagging for what seemed like an eternity. I would then sit myself down on the dirty floor, put my head down on the toilet seat, and just cry my eyes out. I was miserable.

The one symptom I haven't mentioned until now was a little itchy area in my chest. Two years before my initial diagnosis, I was working as a counselor in a camp for special-needs children. I remember waking up one night in the most excruciating pain. It was emanating for this huge bump on my chest. It looked as if one of my ribs had popped out of place. The camp doctor said he'd never seen anything like it and decided to call an ambulance. I was rushed to a very small, sparsely staffed hospital, seemingly in the middle of nowhere. There, I was given a chest x-ray and, it was determined that I had a virus, which was causing the pain and inflammation. I went back to camp. Within a day or two, the swelling had subsided and so had the pain. Only one symptom persisted. There was a little itch inside my chest, but I never thought much of it. It bothered me once in a while, but I adapted to it, like one can adapt to any minor discomfort.

Little did I know that the doctors had misdiagnosed me. Had I been properly diagnosed back then, my life to this day would have played out very differently. My cancer would have been caught right away, and I probably would have just needed a few treatments of radiation. I guess one mustn't go through life thinking if only. It can truly drive you crazy. Yet it was misdiagnosed by those incompetent, barely-passed-the-boards doctors. Anger issues there? Some, yes!

That little "mosquito bite" feeling in my chest never went away. From time to time, I would ask the doctor what it was about, and if it was dangerous. All the doctors had the exact same answer. They didn't know what it was, but it definitely wasn't cancer. As my life went on, I realized how little doctors really know.

Aside from the nausea and hair loss, there was one other major side effect that this ABVD concoction gave me. I struggle with it to this day. It is this undeniable weakness. It shouldn't even be called weakness; there should be a different name for this feeling, because weakness doesn't even begin to describe how you feel. My body felt so weak that it would take every bit of strength just to shuffle to the bathroom, four feet away. My four-foot hike to the bathroom was my cardio workout for the day. When completed, I would need a four-hour nap to recover, only to have to do the whole thing over again when I awoke. It was debilitating and depressing. You start having to rely on people for everything, and I hated that.

I think the scariest part of everything I was going through was the unknown. Is the chemo working? Is the cancer going away? Will it ever come back? You kind of tell yourself, okay, I have to go through this hell (and I mean hell) in order to get myself well and back on track. But I didn't have a crystal ball, so I had no idea if this poison flowing through my body would save me or kill me. If I'd known for sure that everything would be okay at the end, it would have been easier to go through.

At the hospital, the doctors came by to check on me daily. My doctor would always come to me with his army of little doctor-ants that marched behind him. Who gave these little annoying bugs the right to come into my room and see me in this compromised condition? Okay, my doctor had to come in and check my heart and lungs, but why the entourage? Everyone came with their stupid clipboards, and I just wanted them to get out of my room, and let me lay there in peace!

Eventually, I put a sign on my door. It read:

BEWARE!
CRAZY CANCER PATIENT IN ROOM
ENTER AT YOUR OWN RISK.

That was the last time an army doctor-ant walked into my room.

I had no control over what was happening in my life, nor what was happening inside of me. My own body was, in a sense, trying to kill me. Who gave my cells the right to start multiplying like crazy? My cells had a basic job, and that was just to grow and do what they were supposed to do. That should not be too complicated, so why did my cells go haywire?

Then there were the scans and blood tests, and the endless waiting. Don't these technicians know that they are holding life or death information for you? You would think they would forgo their lunch break for ten minutes to give you a quick callback. Maybe I was being selfish, but come on! When the phone rings, is the doctor going to say the tumors have shrunk, or will he say the chemo is not working? Every minute felt like an eternity. I wouldn't wish that suspense on my worst enemy. No one should ever have to wait for a phone call to find out whether he is going to live or die.

We humans are a strange bunch. We know that we are all going to die at some point, but we never really believe it's going to happen to us. I am young, I am strong, I am fine. Coming face-to-face with the possibility of death (or worse: long suffering), is one of the greatest tests of faith. Still, not knowing how long we have actually keeps us going. If God put an expiration date on the heel of every baby who was born, and we knew exactly when we would leave this earth, I think we would go nuts. I personally would be counting down the days, the hours. The fear of the known would handicap me so that I probably would not be able to live a normal life.

My being a cancer patient made me think about my mortality every second of every day, and I was never ready to accept it. No way! I had way too much living to do! Yet even with all the positive thinking in the world, I really had zero control over anything in my life. My grandmother used to say, "You could be the healthiest person in the world. You walk down the street, an air conditioner falls on your head, the end!" Blunt, but true.

I have what they call baby veins. They are tiny and don't like to pop up when they are called upon. These "babies" give me a real rough time. Anyone out there who also has really "shy" veins knows first-hand what a pain in the neck it is to get blood-work done. You start to become a human pin-cushion, and it just is not fun. These technicians don't even care. This is what they do — prick people all day long! I have a general rule when it comes to blood drawing: I allow a one-prick maximum per person. If you don't succeed the first time around, you aren't getting a second chance! These nurses always disliked me. I would sometimes have to endure three or four people trying, until finally someone would hit the bull's eye.

After a few months, my poor veins were done. All that probing and poking caused my veins to "rebel" and collectively decide to withhold their precious red blood. So that put me in a bit of a predicament. How were the doctors supposed to safely monitor me without checking my blood? How was I supposed to receive my intravenous chemotherapy? This is when I began to hear the term catheter. I had no idea what it was but didn't like the sound of it one bit. It was a simple surgical procedure, where under local anesthesia, the doctor inserts a big, ugly, plastic tube into the middle of my chest. It didn't hurt much, but was scary nonetheless. When I looked down, I found this weird plastic hose coming out of my body. It just looked and felt weird. (No more bathing suits for a while!)

I could not get it wet, so in order to shower I had to wrap myself up in tape and saran wrap like last night's leftovers. You would think that in this day and age, the medical community would have come up with something better than plastic wrap. I mean, come on, we sent a man to the moon, and we have satellites that can see the numbers on license plates from space, but you can't figure out a better way than saran wrap and scotch tape to keep my catheter dry?

Three months into my treatment, my doctor sent me for a CT scan to see if the chemo was working. This was my second time on the cold, metal table waiting to be told to breathe in and breathe out. This time, the results were wonderful. The doctor told me that the mass had shrunk to a quarter of its original size. He told me that this was a very good sign. He said that with the kind of Hodgkin's that I had, the stage in which they had caught it, and how quickly the chemotherapy had worked, I had a ninety-eight percent chance of curing this thing. I couldn't believe my ears. You really can't ask for better odds.

I felt like dancing in the streets. I must have hugged the doctor as hard as I could. I did become slightly concerned when he began to turn blue, so I took it down a notch and just gave him a great big smile. I felt like God had given my life back to me, and I was never again going to take it for granted. I was going to appreciate everything, and give my life a purpose.

THE SECRET IS OUT

Now I could finally get back to my Nathaniel. How I went through all of this without telling him is beyond me. Until this day, I have no idea how I was able to manage two separate lives, while going through so much. There were days when I thought I was going to go crazy, but I somehow got it together. I owe so much to my loving parents. They really were the ones who stood by my side through everything, and told me that however I wanted to deal with this, they were on board.

After months of spending time together, I began to love Nathaniel more and more each day. I trusted him and loved everything about him.

I knew it was time for me to tell him my secret. But how do you tell a guy you truly love that everything he knows about you is a lie, and that you've hidden a huge secret from him? Whether I was in the right or wrong for not telling him, I knew now that I had to be honest. I was shaking for days before I told him. Remember, I never thought I would really love anyone, and here was a guy I truly loved. I wanted to spend the rest of my life with him. How should I tell him? Should I start from the beginning or just tell him right away? "Hi Nathaniel, can we talk? I have been hiding something from you since we met. I have cancer". He would think that I was playing some kind of morbid joke or something. No way would he believe me.

Well, it was now or never. I cried a lot that week. I cried for having to be stuck in this horrible situation. I cried for the potential loss that I might suffer and I cried for the unfairness of it all.

Nathaniel came to pick me up at about seven that Saturday

night. I told him that there was something important I wanted to talk to him about. And then I told him everything. It was like a tsunami of information that I just had to release, like helium out of a balloon. If I was going to do this and set the record straight, I had to be honest about all the dishonesty I had been perpetuating for so long. I told him what I'd been diagnosed with, and why I hadn't told him about it all these months. I kept looking at him to see if I could read what he was feeling, but his face was white like a ghost. He was in shock. I knew it, I thought. He'll never want to stay with me. Why would he? Why should he? I felt like I'd become tainted goods. Not only was I defective, but untrustworthy as well! I told him the positive statistics the doctor had shared with me, and that I was in remission now.

His face remained white, and cold as ice. Not knowing what else to do, I started to cry. I thought this was probably the last time I would be seeing the man I cared about most. Who was going to want me after this? Who would ever want to marry me? Why in heaven's name would anyone ever want to choose me? I would be alone for the rest of my life. I would be one of those old ladies who smell of mothballs and take in too many cats. How depressing!

It felt like an eternity, but finally he looked at me and said that he had to go home and process everything I'd just told him. Then he got up and left. I remember that moment like it was yesterday. I remember closing the front door to my parents' home and just collapsing to the floor. My legs just wouldn't hold me up, no matter how hard I tried. I cried like I'd never cried in my life. That was it. I would never know love again. I would never get married or have children. I would be alone forever, branded and marked by my dreadful disease like a leper!

My Nathaniel was something special, I mean really, something special. The next night he showed up at my house. I had no idea what he was going to say, but if he was breaking it off, at least he was doing it in person, like a decent human being. He told me that my news had indeed shocked him. He couldn't believe his ears. He'd been up all night contemplating what to do and how to handle this.

I held my breath as he spoke. Finally, he said, "Emma I am going to stay by your side!" I thought I was hearing things. Had he just said he was going to stay with me? Could it be true? I must have heard him wrong. Maybe my brain was playing tricks on me. But no, he repeated it. He told me that he cared about me deeply, and we would get through things in life together. I felt as though I was in the presence of an angel. Any typical guy might have said, "Adios amiga, I'm out of here". Even the nice ones would have probably bailed. Nathaniel wasn't spooked. I would always have the love of my life by my side.

I thanked God every day for the love Nathaniel and I shared. It was better than in the movies. It was real, pure, and beautiful. I knew how lucky I was to have this gift.

MY FIRST TATTOO

Aﬆ﬇﬇﬈ I'D FINALLY COMPLETED ALL six months, (twelve rounds) of my chemotherapy, I was ready to begin the next phase of my treatment. I couldn't understand why the doctor was still giving me dangerous doses of poison to kill the cancer when after four months, it was all gone. He kept telling me, if there was even one cell out there, he wanted to make sure we zapped it. So for the next two months my father would drive me into the city for radiation treatments. Before my first treatment, the doctor asked me, "Did you ever get a tattoo?" *What does getting a tattoo have to do with the price of tea in China?* I thought. I was then told that in order for the technicians to measure the exact area requiring radiation, the doctors must tattoo a few small areas on my chest. This was yet another way that I'd be branded forever because of this crazy disease. Thus, in June of 1993, I got my first tattoo. Not cool.

It took about fifteen minutes each time to set up the machines in a way that would pinpoint the exact places to target. I didn't feel much after the treatments, except for a little topical sensitivity and some weakness. Unfortunately, that feeling was not new to me.

For eight weeks, I received radiation daily. By summer's end, I was officially done, officially in remission. *This nightmare is almost over*, I encouraged myself. *I can see the light at the end of the tunnel! I can finally begin to heal and take care of myself. I can resume college classes and normal life!*

Boy, was I ever wrong.

Over the next six months, Nathaniel and I enjoyed many wonderful moments. We were blissfully in love. It was the real deal. We would die for one another and we both knew it. There is a closeness that comes from going through difficult times with someone you love. There is a bond that could never have been created without that united suffering. Nathaniel was one of my greatest blessings from God. His love was like receiving a new gift every single day.

This part of my life played out like an epic movie. I could close my eyes, and think about a particular song we both liked, or other great memories of us together. It was my little movie, my little slide show. Little did I know then how much more suffering was in store for me and the love of my life.

It was time for my six-month CT scan. This was simply to ensure that the cancer had not returned — that I was still in remission.

I'd just finished my morning classes, and decided to call my father at work to see if he'd heard any news from the doctor. The tone of my father's voice indicated something was wrong. He told me he was on his way to pick me up. Why was he picking me up? I always took the bus. Why couldn't I take the bus today?

The minute I sat down beside him, my poor father, who could hardly face me, mumbled, "Emma the cancer is back." The scan had shown another small mass in my chest — more Hodgkins. Are you kidding me? Are you for real? How could this be happening? My story already had a beginning, a middle, and an end! I had neither emotional nor physical space for another chapter, let alone a sequel! NO, NO, NO!

My father had more bad news, and he didn't mince words. He told me that chemotherapy alone was not an option anymore, since previous high doses clearly hadn't done the trick. The only option I actually had of curing this thing was to endure a bone marrow transplant. I had no idea what that was. Was it like having a heart transplant? Was I going to have to borrow some dead person's bone marrow in order to save my life? My father reminded me of the procedure I'd undergone a year before. The doctor had extracted some of my bone marrow while I was in remission. So, like a tax refund, I'd actually be getting back my own marrow. This would eliminate many common problems that can occur during a bone marrow transplant. It is much safer to reabsorb your own marrow than that of another person. I remember asking the doctor why I would have to go through that whole procedure if there was a ninety-eight percent chance of no recurrence? His response was, "We do it for the two percent". I guess someone has to be the two percent. This time, it was me.

So this bone marrow thing, it would entail my being in the hospital for over a month. However, before this month of hell begins, you are given very strong chemo drugs, to ensure eradication of any lingering cancer cells. The goal is to launch your bone marrow transplant with your body in a state of full remission.

After the initial chemo was over, I would enter a second hospital, which would inter me for the next month or so during my bone marrow transplant. During this time, I was told, the doctors would inject me with chemotherapy agents strong enough to wipe out my whole immune system. At the same time, their hope was that it would wipe out any stubborn cancer cells that were cruel enough to try hiding in small, obscure places. So now this lethal chemotherapy would be the strongest my body could handle and still survive.

This was a dangerous thing that I was about to endure. My body, still weak and recovering from the first bout of poison I'd received not too long ago, was about to get tackled with another much more lethal dose. Would I survive it? Not everybody does. There is a lot of risk. More than I ever wanted to think about.

Then came the most devastating news of all. Due to the extreme doses of chemotherapy, all my eggs would be destroyed. No, I don't mean my organic eggs in the fridge next to the skim milk. I mean eggs that a female is born with, which eventually become your children! The children you live your life for, the legacy you leave behind after you are gone. **In order to beat the cancer, I would have to give up the chance of ever having my own children.**

That was it. I couldn't take it anymore. It felt like someone was dumping cement on me! How could this be happening? God was now taking away my ability to ever give birth to children. I couldn't bear it. Broken-hearted, I started screaming at my father, "Who is ever going to want me now? I will always be alone, no marriage, no children!" Everything was being ripped away from me, and it was all happening so fast. And how was I going to tell Nathaniel?

This time I was too afraid and too broken to tell him myself. Even an angel would leave me now, I thought sadly. So I asked my father to break the news.

After about an hour, my father finally came upstairs, and said, "Honey, you are in love with someone extremely special, and he wants to see you." I walked downstairs, afraid to see Nathaniel's face. Nathaniel stared into my eyes, and said to me, "I told you before, I am with you no matter what. We will get through this together, and we are going to be okay!" Naturally, I started crying. I had so many emotions pent-up inside of me. On the one hand, I was on the cusp of a new battle to save my life. On the other hand, I was so incredibly lucky to have found Nathaniel. I was living the greatest love story that could ever have been written. This man was willing to give up everything for me. He was my silver lining.

THE TRANSPLANT

THE GOLD-EMBOSSED PLAQUE ON THE door read: Infertility Specialists of New York. My doctor had advised me to increase and store my eggs before the transplant. So I began treatments to try to increase my egg supply by taking daily hormone shots.

Nathaniel accompanied me to all my visits. He would sit with me in the waiting room trying to find words to cheer me up. I remember vividly watching couples gazing at the angelic baby pictures pinned all along the clinic's "success wall". I was so envious. Their problems were big, don't get me wrong, but my problem was so much bigger. I was battling a life-threatening disease at the same time. My anxiety made the shots hurt that much more. The constant blood-work and doctor visits began to wear me down. I was losing patience and I'd just about had enough.

After I'd finally finished all the injections, the doctor grimly informed me that only four viable eggs had been produced. The chances of my getting pregnant with these four eggs was five percent. Five percent! And the cost of first retrieving those eggs (to freeze for future use) was over ten thousand dollars. I was overwhelmed with disappointment. Nathaniel and I discussed it and decided to forego the whole egg saga and focus on my getting cured. I had tried. I'd really, really tried, but it seemed that nothing I was doing was working. Nothing was going my way. I would look up at the sky and cry to God. I would ask him why He was doing this to me. I begged Him to give me the strength to persevere.

I'd always had a close relationship with God, even as a child. I thought of him as a protective Father who would help and guide me though life unconditionally. Never in a million years did I imagine that He would allow all of this to happen to me. However, my faith was strong and complete. I knew at the end, my life would improve and He would bless me with good fortune. I believed that God was giving me these near-impossible life trials to earn what He was saving for me-a life filled with health, happiness, peace, and longevity. I had to deserve my prize, and going through all of this was the way God had set up my reward system.

This time around, I couldn't keep it a secret. I had to tell my extended family, my friends, my world, that I was suffering from this dreadful disease. It was at that point that I started to experience the "I feel so bad for you and I'm so relieved not to be in your shoes" look, as well as the pity look, the awkward look, the I-don't-know-what-to-say-so-of-course-I-am-going-to-say-something-stupid look. It took me a very long time to get used to those faces, and I still have trouble with them to this day. The things that would come out of people's mouths were rarely helpful. I could write a whole book on what *not* to say to someone who has cancer. You would be shocked at the absolute simplicity of some people. People would say things like, "You know that God only gives you tests that you can handle, right?" Are you flipping kidding me? People who say things like that are either very lucky, never having gone through anything too terrible, or people who are just plain fools. God does sometimes give people things that they can't handle. Life is not always "fair" and good people often suffer. But I believe deep down that He loves us all very much. Why does He test or punish us with trials that seem impossible? I don't know. All I know is that I don't have any choice in the matter. I was put on this earth for a purpose. I can either wile away my days complaining and being depressed about my lot, or I can enrich my life thanking God for every little amazing thing that He has given me. This, I do have a choice about! It is not easy. Don't get me wrong, there are plenty of mornings when I just don't want to get out of bed. I don't always have the strength to deal with what life is offering me at the moment. But again, what are the choices? So I get up and brush myself off, yet again.

It was time for me to begin my second battle with this disease. My initial phase of treatment was the two week hospital stay, where I was infused with three chemo agents called ICE. Unfortunately, this treatment had nothing to do with an ice slushy from 7-Eleven. This was a strong combination of chemotherapy drugs that would hopefully put me back into remission. After two weeks of ICE, my CT scan showed the mass was gone. Now it was up to the bone marrow transplant to kill off any resistant cells that might be lurking around in the shadows.

The next phase was my one month hospital stay where I was to receive the bone marrow transplant. I came armed with one hundred of my favorite pictures. I would make sure to hang them all over my wall, so when the hard times came, I could look around and see all the wonderful times I'd had, and remember that please God, the best was yet to come. There is one thing that I found to be true of any hospital. As a patient, you tend to become "a room number" to the medical staff. You are no longer a human being with a first and last name, with feelings and a real life. Dealing with mass numbers of sick people, many nurses and doctors become numb to it all. I would no longer be Emma Harot, the fun loving, twenty-one year old girl from New York. From here on, I would be Room #807 Bed #2.

I knew this was going to be my home for quite a while, and that my chances of survival depended greatly on the care of these nurses day in and day out. I needed to make myself different in order to survive. I needed to remind them that the girl in Bed #2 is a human being. She has a life outside this hospital room. So the first thing I did upon entering my "suite" was decorate the wall, floor to ceiling with all my photographs. I believe the nurses were extra gentle with me because of my special "wall mural". I wouldn't let them forget that I was still part of their species. I was just like them.

I don't remember much of the month that I spent on the bone marrow transplant floor. I think the brain blocks out memories that are just too painful, in order to keep you sane. I do remember that Nathaniel came every day to see me. He breathed life into me when there was not much left.

The intense chemotherapy regimen started right away. The doctors didn't give me any time to get adjusted. This was WAR, war with my cancer cells! The medications made me so sick. My hair was short, still growing back from the initial chemotherapy treatments, but it was cute and curly. This time, my hair fell out right away. It was like everything I'd gone through the year before, only ten times stronger and faster. I have no idea how I survived it.

I made some friends on the floor; a group of us that had different forms of cancer, but all doing the best we could to survive. Some of my new friends did very well, and were discharged after the predetermined schedule of treatments. However, not all my "bone marrow buddies" made it out okay.

Some of them left their rooms due to major complications and never came back. I never asked where they'd gone. I never wanted to know. I was too scared of the answer, so I just focused on the ones who were still with me.

My grandmother helped me throughout this time as well. The consecutive sleepless nights were hard on my parents, yet someone had to be with me around the clock. My grandmother left my grandfather alone for the first time in sixty years and came up north to help take care of her sick granddaughter. I remember one night feeling such unbearable nausea. I kept calling desperately for the nurse to give me some relief. The facility was understaffed, and no one ever came. But I had a secret weapon: Grandma!

She was a 4 foot 9 inch elderly woman who possessed the strength of six horses. She would wash her floors on hands and knees and would never consider using a paper plate ("A waste!" she would say). If there were more people in this world who thought like my grandma, there would be a lot more trees in the rainforest today.

After hearing me scream "Nurse!" for ten minutes, Grandma ran out of my room screaming at the top of her lungs, "My granddaughter needs help!" She wouldn't stop running up and down the ward like a crazy person until she got someone to come into my room and give me something for the nausea. That was my grandmother, and I think I am a lot like her. She was probably the toughest person I'd ever known.

After a few weeks of chemotherapy, my immune system was basically at zero, and it was time for the bone marrow transfer. This new bone marrow would hopefully re-infuse my weakened body with life-giving and healthy blood. I waited for it to be scheduled.

I was given no warning on that particular day. So I was shocked when a group of doctors came into my room, wearing white gowns, gloves, and masks. They told me they were ready to inject my bone marrow. I was not mentally prepared for this. I was alone in my room without any of my family members to hold my hand through this horribly painful procedure. I remember screaming like an animal. I don't remember anything up to that point in my life that was as painful as that. I was left in my room alone, so exhausted on every level that I really wasn't sure if I was going to live. Truthfully at that point I almost didn't care if I did. That was one of the lowest points in my life.

As time went on, though, things began to look brighter, and I began to feel better with each passing day. Both red and white blood cell counts were beginning to rise, and my platelet count went from non-existent to safer, healthy levels in a matter of weeks. Finally the day came. I was allowed to go home. Free at last!

As I was packing my things and peeling my creased pictures off the wall, I felt the "mosquito bite" inside my chest again. I asked the transplant doctor, and he said the same thing that every other doctor had said before. It had nothing to do with my cancer. I wanted to believe the doctors so much. I had to believe them. I could not fathom how a single cancer cell could have possibly survived the chemo holocaust my body had endured.

It took a few months for my body and soul to begin to feel alive again. Nathaniel and I decided that we'd waited long enough. It was time to celebrate our love and survival together, through it all.

We were married on February 5, 1994. The hall was streaming with friends and family, excited to share in this magical moment. I was marrying the man of my dreams. I had overcome the Big C, and my normal life was finally going to begin. We loved each other more than life itself, and I knew God was going to be good to me. I had earned it!

We moved into a cozy little apartment. I spent my days trying to finish up my master's degree and my evenings cooking delicious meals for my new husband. I had so much love to give him, and I put it all into my food. He loved it, and he loved me. We were truly happy.

One night, I decided to meet some friends in the city for dinner. I was not a drinker, but I did like the occasional girly drink topped with of course, a frilly paper toothpick umbrella. We were having a good time, when suddenly I felt a sharp stabbing pain in my chest. I didn't know what was happening to me. I went to the ladies' room as calmly as I could. I must have stayed there for almost an hour, until the pain finally dissipated. My friends were worried about me and asked if I was all right. I said that I was fine, just not feeling well and that I had better head home. I was nervous, because I'd never felt anything like that pain before and it was in my chest, my danger zone. The next week I went to the top Hodgkin's specialist in the city and told him my fruity-drink story. His faced just dropped, and he said we should run some tests to make sure all was okay. I agreed, but I began to learn how to read people, and this was an easy read. **This guy knew. He just knew.**

What I found out later is that Hodgkin's cells dislike alcohol. Who hates alcohol? Who gives these stupid, unwanted cells a right to like or dislike anything? However, when I told him that this episode happened right after I'd finished drinking my alcoholic beverage, he immediately understood what was going on.

I went for my umpteenth CT scan, and waited and prayed that I was okay. The scans showed that the cancer had come back, again. This time, it was deeply embedded in the bone tissue of my sternum.

Nathaniel was the one who had to impart this news to me. His car pulled up in the driveway midday, and I knew the news was bad. He didn't have to say a word.

My mind went wild. *I can't go through one more thing! I won't go through one more thing!*

I took my car keys, ran out of the apartment, and just drove away. I could see Nathaniel in my rear-view mirror, frantically waving as he ran behind the car, begging me to stop.

I wanted to run away from my reality. I just drove and drove, for hours on end. I had no idea where I was going, but I had to go somewhere. I had to run away from the disastrous news that threatened to crush me to my core. So I kept driving, crying, and screaming all at the same time.

I screamed, "God, how could you do this to me? After everything you've put me through? I never asked to be born! I never asked to live! You put me here on this earth only to make me suffer? Where is your compassion? You are supposed to be my Father and Protector!" I felt betrayed by Him. All the love and trust that I'd always had in God was shaken by this unexpected news.

After a few hours of driving, I realized something. Where could I go to hide? Where could I go to get away from this?

Wherever I went, my body would ultimately follow. Physically, I couldn't run away from myself. Defeated, I decided to drive home. I think a big part of me gave up at that moment. I was done fighting. I was done with chemotherapy. I was done with everything. I was just done, done, DONE! This dreadful disease had won. With all my fighting, it still somehow beat me by a landslide. I didn't care what happened to me at that point.

"Please, just don't let me suffer anymore," I pleaded with Nathaniel. His gentle reassurance gave me some measure of inner peace. I remember sleeping well that night.

We went to a top-notch lymphoma specialist in Sloan-Kettering Hospital, New York. I was told the only way to beat this was to endure another bone marrow transplant. That would give me a fifty percent chance of remission. The doctor began his speech with statistics, but statistics meant nothing to me.

"No," I said emphatically. "I will not go through the terror and agony of that again."

Relatives and friends tried to sway my decision, but no one could change my mind. I would never ever put my body and soul through "treatments" again. Never! I would rather die, I told them. And I meant it.

God blessed me with parents that were simply the best. My father spent the next decade scouting out clinical trials, experimental theories and more. We tried almost every far-fetched idea out there. Some of them were unusual (to say the least), and some were medically based, but you name it, we tried it.

My father was amazing through all of this. If not for him, I wouldn't have made it this far. He was and still is my rock. No matter what, he always reassured me that he would not let anything bad happen to me. He told me that if I didn't like what one doctor had to say, we would find another until I was satisfied.

"We will go to the ends of the earth to make sure you live a happy, healthy, long life," Dad promised. I believed him and still do. His positive attitude was a huge part of my story.

The first thing we had to tackle was finding a surgeon who would be willing to follow *my* suggestion: excise the affected section of my sternum, and replace it with a prosthetic of some kind.

Every doctor said the same thing. Lymphoma is a systemic disease and it cannot be cured by surgery. They were right. But I had to think out-of-the-box. Maybe the next year, they would come up with a miraculous drug to combat this disease, and I just had to wait until that time. I had no idea. All I knew was that I needed to do something drastic, unrelated to chemotherapy.

The first few doctors we approached refused to operate; it was just too dangerous. Most doctors were afraid to touch me with a ten-foot pole.

All except Dr. Bahami.

"You can't fix it, but if you remove it, won't that buy me some time?" I asked.

He looked at my scans and said, "I think I can do this

surgery for you. It will be very complicated, but I think it can be done".

Finally, we'd found someone daring enough to operate on me. I felt a surge of happiness course through me. I had some control finally, and I would continue to make these decisions from now on.

OUTSMARTING THE LITTLE DEVILS

I HAD TO OUTSMART THOSE devilish cancer cells. They had learned how to hide from the most destructive poisons the medical world was hurling at them.

Originally, all I could think of was "Cure me!" but once I realized that nothing was working, I decided I was done with that goal. My new mantra was "**I decide what happens to this body of mine!**" I stopped blindly trusting the doctors, and started trusting myself more. I was going to run the show. I was going to say what could and could not be done to my body. I had to be creative, and I hoped God was on my side, but I'd defined my new goal: KEEP THE CANCER AT BAY. I realized that these annoying creatures might be with me for a while, but we would control them as best as we could. When the cells would be on to what I was doing, I would have to switch tactics and try something else. I had to be one step ahead of them, always. This was not going to be a fast and furious war, with a beginning and an end. I realized that my struggle with cancer was about *many* battles. Some I would lose and some I would win.

My Hodgkin's had never responded predictably to anything. The cells seemed to "bounce back" even after months of chemotherapy, radiation, and a full-blown bone marrow transplant. But at this point, they were reproducing slowly, which gave me a greater chance of overpowering them. I had to become my own doctor. I had to be on top of my game. I had these little mini-explosives inside my body, determined to destroy me! Admittedly, living like that is exhausting, both physically and emotionally. To be at battle constantly wore me down. But I refused to put up my little white flag and surrender! That was my firm decision. I would fight and fight, until these cells were so sick of battling me that one day they would give up. I didn't know when it would happen, but I had to believe that it would. Just like dawn follows the night, God would make sure that this unfair battle would have a happy ending. Good would outwit evil.

The day of my surgery finally arrived. It was hours long, and the recovery was even harder. I was in a tremendous amount of pain. I remember having this pain-relief-release button on the side of my hospital bed. Whenever the pain was unbearable, I would press the button and would get a dose of something that would give me immediate relief. I don't know what they were giving me, but whatever it was worked. It is just not fair that the only time you get these mind-numbing drugs is when you are too sick to enjoy them. I would love a dose of whatever I got then, once a week now!

The surgeons looked over the biopsied cells and told me that my "margins were clean". Dr. Bahami had incised the sick and damaged tissue from the chest and sternum and replaced it with a synthetic mesh of some kind. It was an odd feeling knowing that I had this paper-like mesh thing holding up my body, but it was doing the trick so I didn't complain.

Now, many oncologists believe that cancer does not have to be annihilated by insane doses of chemo which destroy the body's good cells as well. There are times when it is appropriate to "go in for the kill" and other times when it is smarter to view the disease as a chronic illness.

Over the next decade or so, I did not visit one traditional oncologist. I know everybody thought I was irresponsible. Even the surgeons (whom I convinced to operate on me) thought I was one card short of a full deck. I didn't care what anyone thought. I knew I would be my own best doctor. No one knew my body as well as I did. So this was how I lived a big chunk of my life.

The Hodgkin's cells were still in my body. Every few months I would get a lump here and a bump there. I would go to different surgeons and ask them to literally cut it out. I did my own thing for a full decade and my cancer was kept at bay which had been my goal all along.

I went through several chest surgeries. Those beasts were having a fiesta on me, but as long as they didn't go near any major organs or make me feel sick, I let them do whatever they wanted. I "bought" myself many years of chemo-free life to enjoy with my family. On the average of once a year, I would have pieces of affected muscle and skin taken out, so long as the doctors confirmed I could survive without those parts.

At that time in my life, I tried everything, and I mean everything, to beat these crummy cancer cells of mine without chemotherapy. My father and I took a trip to Florida to visit a well-known energy healer. He taught me the art of meditation and self-healing the body. It was a bit kooky, but I was willing to try anything once.

I began reading a book about one woman's journey of survival with ovarian cancer. She'd switched to a macrobiotic diet, which basically means eating whole grains, freshly cooked veggies and seaweed, exclusively. This diet cured her, so I thought maybe it could do the same for me.

The next week I signed up for a local macrobiotic cooking class and learned how to change my whole way of eating. I ate truckloads of brown rice and spent the next two years of my life cooking healthy macrobiotic food. Everything had to be fresh, organic, and cooked that same day. It became my full time job. Understandably, my dear husband refused to eat what he called my "rabbit food". He is what you call a meat-and-potatoes kind of guy, and my diet was the polar opposite of the way he liked to eat. So not only was I cooking for myself up to half a day, but I also had to cook different meals for Nathaniel as well. For two years, I was in the kitchen; chopping, cooking and following a horrible-tasting macrobiotic diet.

At the same time, I frequented a Chinese healer. I went into Chinatown to get specific herbs, guaranteed to heal. I soon learned that these herbs were major diuretics! So now my day consisted of cooking, and endless visits to the restroom. It was no fun at all.

I began to receive treatments from a special acupuncturist. He inserted hundreds of little needles all over my body, which he then attached to some kind of electrical machine. After he flipped the switch on this old black box, every one of those needles started pulsating with crazy-strong electric shocks. A few needles meant a few shocks. But try it with one hundred needles, stuck to every part of your body! He was definitely a quack. But I was crazier, because I actually went back to him a few times and continued to allow him to literally electrocute me. I guess if you are willing to try almost anything, you will eventually meet up with some nut cases. I haven't been to Chinatown ever since. I began researching vitamin drips and all kinds of other alternative treatments. I figured it couldn't hurt. Whatever was out there, I tried. The one treatment I continued with for over a decade was my once-a-week intravenous vitamin drips. Over a four hour period, I would be injected with very high doses of vitamin C and other anti-cancer agents. Every year or so, another alternative non-toxic treatment would be added to the mix. I wasn't picky. They could have put in last's night's dinner, I wouldn't have known. I figured the more the merrier.

At first, I started going to the Atkins Center in midtown Manhattan. I remember meeting Dr. Atkins for the first time. He was an older, distinguished-looking fellow who was as healthy as a horse. He was a successfully published author, had his own radio talk show, and a whole line of Atkins' vitamins and food products. The guy was at the top of his game. I became a regular at his clinic, and the nurses and Atkins team knew me well. I would drive into the city early in the morning (for classes I was still attempting to finish), then take the subway to the Atkins Center for my weekly drips. I met with Dr. Atkins, and he proposed a basic regimen for me. Every so often, he would find out about a new alternative treatment that was just approved by the FDA and didn't mind testing it out on little ol' me. I remember this one shot that I *almost* received called 714X. It was supposed to help in the fight to destroy my cancer cells, so how could I possibly say no? The nurse came in with a needle the size of Kentucky! Then she proceeded to tell me how and where this shot would be administered. It had to be injected in the groin area. Somehow, I consented. All I can say is: this shot was not intended for humans. The pain was so beyond intense, that whatever was in the syringe never had a fighting chance of making it into my body. I screamed so loud that I really think I emptied out the whole third-floor clinic. When I went to pay my bill, there was not one person left on my wing. That was the first and last time the center tried 714X on me.

The cost of these drips was a small fortune. I had no idea why a little bag of vitamin C would cost close to three hundred dollars. I kept thinking about how many pair of shoes I would have loved to buy with all that money. But insurance would not cover a thing. The only treatment my wonderful health insurance would cover was the cost of the chemotherapy and hospital stays. Non-standard treatments were not considered acceptable protocol by the insurance companies.

Don't even get me started with the absolute corruptness of these companies. I understand that it is all a business, but the blatant lying and dishonesty that goes along with the whole industry is stomach-turning. My mother would spend hours and hours on the phone with these companies, trying to obtain information necessary for reimbursement. They would tell her that they "sent the information in the mail" when they never did. Insurance companies are meant to help the sick. What ill person has the energy it takes to play the games you have to play to be reimbursed? Unfortunately, the insurance companies will do anything NOT to pay out your claim. Most people give up. Thank heaven, I have my mom, who never gives up. She hounded them day and night, for many years. Ultimately they relented and paid.

One morning on my way to class, as I was sitting in bumper-to-bumper traffic, listening to the radio, I heard someone on the station talking about Dr. Atkins. At first I thought they were going to mention some new line of his products now on the market. The reporter said that Dr. Atkins had died. I couldn't believe it. What had happened to my strong-as-a-horse, fit-as-a-fiddle doctor? He was the epitome of health. I think it all comes back to my grandmother's saying about the air conditioner: No one knows what fate has in store for them. All this time, Dr. Atkins was so careful. He was treating hundreds if not thousands of sick patients. He had one of the biggest lines of vitamins and health care products out there, and then one winter day, he left the clinic and slipped on a piece of ice. He hit his head on the concrete and was pronounced dead by the end of the day. I couldn't believe it. I thought to myself, you just never know. Everything is in God's hands. The saying that man plans and God laughs really is true.

Over the years, I traveled to all kinds of crazy places and met some really "interesting" people, who did all kinds of unusual things to me. There was one woman who was supposed to have some kind of healing powers. I decided to make an appointment to see her. I remember arriving at her home. Her apartment smelled like bitter herbs and smelly feet. She told me to sit down, and began brewing up a "special" tea just for me. I love tea, but then she brought me a cup of her "tea". It was black. Not coffee-black, but thick-mud black. I can't even describe the smell, but trust me, it was not something that you would want to taste or even inhale. Maybe I could have taken some and fixed my shoe, or put it in the soil to help plants grow. But to drink this thick, black goop? Okay, it was for my health. In one breath, I chugged the entire thing. Almost instantly, my stomach started rumbling and making sounds it had never made before. I think it was telling me, you idiot, what did you do? What a mess! Now I have to figure out how to get rid of this stuff! The Voodoo

Lady just smiled, happy that I had finished her healing tea. Then she asked me to lie down on her dusty living room floor. Now I was thinking: What was I doing this time? I was trying to remember which friend had referred me to this eccentric lady. I made a mental note to egg her house when I was done with this completely creepy woman. Then she began to climb on my back with her feet, and walk up and down the length of my body. Was she crazy? She was short but skinny she was not! I was in so much pain. What did she think she was doing taking a walk, up and down my spine, as if I were a sidewalk? Get off of me! But I didn't say anything. I was afraid of her. If she had any kind of healing powers, I didn't want to get her upset and cast a spell on me. I wasn't taking any chances. After she walked her marathon on my back, she told me finally that I could get up. She then asked me for a ludicrous amount of money for her twenty minutes of T&T (Tea & Torture), and said goodbye. That was it. I have no idea what that lady did, but nothing about it seemed kosher to me. Crazy Lady would not be revisited. I would quickly move on to whatever idea my father had finished researching online.

I began seeing a new doctor, Dr. Chan. His office was about an hour and a half drive from my house. He was located in Brooklyn, New York, and I had heard amazing things about him. He was one of the rare doctors who believed in incorporating Chinese medicine into traditional Western medicine. He was always going to medical conferences in Europe to find out the latest new drugs that had just been approved. You could receive many different treatment options in Europe because their FDA system was not as discerning as ours in the United States.

I liked the idea of combining everything together. Now I could go to a doctor who would treat me holistically. I decided to go for a consultation. He was a very kind man and had a great, optimistic attitude that I found contagious. So I began receiving a four-hour IV treatment every week. Half the time, I had no idea what was in those IV bags. I knew Dr. Chan was always trying different alternate methods to beat this cancer thing. I was on board, willing to be his guinea pig. I knew that nothing he would give me would make me sick, and I trusted him completely. I don't know if any of his treatments really helped me, but I just kept trying. I didn't know where my salvation would come from, but I believed that God was good, and he would take care of me in the long run. Through all these roads that I had been traveling, I always felt that He was right by my side whispering in my ear, "My dear one, you will see, at the end, all will be okay. You have to trust me." And I did. I really did put my full trust in Him.

One day, after about a year of Dr. Chan's treatments, I remember entering his office, only to find all the nurses crying at their desks. They informed me that the doctor had some medical issues and had died in his sleep. I couldn't believe it. Young Dr. Chan, the man who was trying to help thousands of sick people, had died. I started crying too, for Dr. Chan, for all his patients who would be lost without him, and for the craziness of this upside-down world we live in.

The oncologist from my initial transplant had passed away, Dr. Atkins had died, and now my wonderful Dr. Chan was gone. My doctors were dropping like flies!

My father began to warn any doctor who wanted to take me on as a patient that his daughter was dangerous. "She killed off all her doctors!" he'd say to them. Once again, I realized that no one is indestructible. Life is so precious, and no one really knows how long God will give them to walk on this earth.

BABIES EVERYWHERE

NATHANIEL AND I WERE MARRIED for five years. As time went on, our friends began starting their own families. When you don't have children and can't have children, the whole world looks like one huge nursery. Babies are everywhere you turn. Wherever I went, it seemed like baby carriages were following me, poking fun, teasing me mercilessly. Wherever I turned, there would be another pregnant woman complaining about how tired she was and how she was ready to burst. I wanted to be ready to burst, too. It wasn't jealousy. I really did want my friends to be happy. But I wanted to be part of the joy as well. It just didn't seem fair to me. Here I was, a woman with so much love to give, who would give anything to be a mother, and it was all taken away from me at such a young age. I yearned deeply to have a family of my own! A big family!

After much pondering and agonizing, I eventually decided that if God had closed one door, perhaps I was meant to open another. I was determined to be a mom.

Nathaniel and I discussed adoption as a good possibility for us. My life until now had been focused on trying to get what I wanted, no matter what. Okay, so my eggs were messed up, so what! I had to be strong, and I had to be creative. Now was the time. So I began to do my research, and found out that it's really not that simple to adopt a baby. It's actually a rather difficult process, and by no means are you assured of becoming a mother at the end of all the phone calls, paperwork, and money spent.

We started out with a lawyer, whom one of my mother's friends had recommended. She told us that we needed to choose a woman from specific states, because adoption laws differ from state to state. Some states give the birth-mother up to a month to change her mind and decide to keep her baby, while other states give only twenty-four hours. Therefore, we had to be very selective about where our potential birth mother would be residing. I'd read too many books and seen too many films about women who adopted babies, developed a loving bond with the child, and then had them cruelly taken away. There is always that risk when it comes to adoption. I wanted to limit the amount of risk. We began writing ads in various newspapers. The concept of reaching out for adoption in this way was hard for me to come to terms with. It was unfairly humbling. I had to essentially sell myself to the reader, proving somehow that I would be the best choice of mother to her unborn baby. Nathaniel and I had to beg someone for their baby.

Hi, my name is Emma Harot. I am a fun-loving woman whose hobbies include photography and hiking. I am smart and sincere and would be a great mom to your baby.

I did it though. I did it over and over again, for months at a time. Our bank account began to dwindle. We spent hours with potential birthmothers, only to find out (a few months later) that they had changed their minds, and wanted to keep their babies. It was a very difficult process.

My mother also helped me research the international adoption process, and we found a lawyer who came highly recommended. I got in touch with the attorney, who began to explain how the whole international adoption process works. It is beyond complicated.

You would think, okay, there are babies out there who have no home, no mother, no father. Then there are couples here in the United States who would jump at the chance to take care of this little baby and give it a good life. So, what's the problem?

Unfortunately, you're dealing with a lot of bureaucracy. It is the children who suffer most from all the ridiculous laws and regulations, which makes it extremely difficult to adopt a child from another country. Some countries require you to wait a few years in order to take your child home with you. Others make it virtually impossible. So despite many generous checks to our lawyer, we had to wait like everyone else. I would call him often, and ask why it was taking so long. His answer was always the same: "We have to get through the red tape. It takes time."

It was a cool December evening when our lawyer finally called us. A newborn baby had been left in the hospital by the birthmother. With no family or information on the child, the hospital contacted our lawyer and asked him to find an adoptive family for him.

Our baby boy was arriving at JFK airport at 8:00 pm the following evening! "Make sure to bring a car seat," advised the lawyer. We had less than twenty-four hours to prepare for this momentous event, but trust me, I was not complaining. The next morning, Nathaniel and I drove to ToysR Us, and started off in Aisle 1. We had no information about our new addition and we had no idea what a baby needed, so we bought everything!

I went to the diaper section and realized you just can't buy diapers, because they come in different sizes. I asked the woman standing next to me for advice. She asked me how old the baby was. I said that I was not sure. Then she asked me how much the baby weighed, and my response was, again, that I was not sure. She looked confused. How could I not know these basic things about my baby? All I knew was that by 8:00 pm that night, I would be driving home with my baby in the backseat. So I decided to buy every single size and brand of diapers, and almost everything else that ToysR Us sells. I had no idea what a breast pump was, but it sounded interesting, so I bought a bunch of those, too. By the end of aisle 12, we had three full carts of baby stuff that we had no idea what we were going to do with, but, it was the most fun shopping spree I ever had. We were on such a high. In a few hours, we would become parents. In a few hours, our lives would change forever.

We waited for quite some time at JFK's International Terminal. We met our lawyer there, and the three of us watched as the flight we'd been awaiting for finally arrived, and passengers began to disembark. The lawyer began talking to a young woman, holding a baby wrapped in a large pink baby blanket. Could that be our baby... boy? This baby was wrapped and covered in pink! The woman smiled at us, said congratulations, and just like that, handed us this little bundle. I kept wondering if the baby was a boy or a girl. I had to know, so I quickly peeked under the fluffy blanket-which incidentally, smelled of spoiled milk and stale airplane air, and quickly popped one of the snaps of the soiled pink onesie. I had a beautiful, odorous baby boy, covered in pink. I later found out that many cultures do not differentiate between baby girls and baby boys when it comes to color. You live and learn.

As we left the airport terminal we began heading toward

my parents' house, so they could teach us how to care for the baby. Small detail: We had decided not to tell anyone as of yet, not even our parents! We didn't want to "jinx" it. We also thought it would be amusing if we just showed up at their door and screamed "Surprise!" and that is exactly what we did. I told my mother that we were going to the airport to pick up a client (which is something we did quite frequently), and then come by for dinner. Nothing out of the ordinary. We pulled up in front of the house, and rang the doorbell. My mother answered the door. I told her to close her eyes, that we had a surprise for her. She decided to play our game and closed her eyes. Never in her wildest dreams did she imagine what was going to happen next. We brought the baby to her arms and said," Open your eyes, Grandma!"

My mother is a woman with a loud voice. But never, in all my years, did I hear this lady shriek the way she did. She kept asking us whose baby this really was, and not to play games with her. I told her that this was no game.

"This is really your first grandchild, Mom," I said softly. "Congratulations!"

Then the screaming started again. We brought our new little pink bundle into the house. "The first thing we need to do is give this kid a bath!" my mother declared. Swiftly, she undressed the little guy and plopped him into the kitchen sink. After he was bathed, she wrapped him in a clean white towel. He was like a shiny new penny. It was then that we heard the car beep from the garage, which meant that my father was home from work. Now we'd enjoy surprising him as well. I told him to come into my old room, where I had a present for him. "Hello, Grandpa," I said as he opened the door. He was shocked. I told my father that it was my baby. My own baby!

For two weeks, we stayed in my parents' home, learning how to take care of a newborn. By the end of that time, Nathaniel was beyond ready to go home. I was nervously wondering if I was ready to do this solo. I didn't want to drop the baby or forget to feed him. I had many pets, and none of them had made it past the three-week mark. I couldn't even keep a cactus alive. I think I watered it to death. So you understand my concerns. We brought our baby home, and we named him after my husband's father, who had passed away some time ago. His name was Louis. Little Louis is what we called him. It was a time of pure bliss for me. I quickly learned how to take care of a baby, and enjoyed every little nuance and detail. **I loved being a mom.** I loved sitting in my new mommy rocking chair, while feeding him his bottle. I loved putting him to sleep. I loved burping him. I loved everything about this little guy.

When Louis was six months old, I began to notice that he was not reaching the typical milestones for a child of that age. He began to cry more often, and it became increasingly difficult to keep soothing him. **They say every cloud has a silver living, but this silver lining had a cloud.**

Louis was getting tougher as time went on. I just kept making excuses for him. We began our nightly ritual of driving him up and down the block while he would fall asleep. This allowed us a few minutes of peace and quiet. That would do the trick, but as soon as we took him out of his car seat, the wailing would begin again.

The poor guy spit up everything and anything he ate. I asked my mother if this spit-up stage was ever going to end. She told me that I could trust her, by the time he was fifteen, he would not be spitting up over my shoulder. She was right about that. But she was wrong about many other things concerning my son.

About a year after we'd adopted our son, (before Louis' subsequent evaluation) we got another unexpected phone call from the same lawyer. He informed us of a baby girl in desperate need of a good home. She was about six months old, with nowhere to go. If she stayed in her country of birth, she would end up living in an orphanage with barely enough food. Could we take her in?

How could I say no to that? I knew it was soon, a bit too soon, but in life you can't always plan. In a perfect world, I would have waited another year until I knew the status with Louis. But who knew if in a year or two, there would be another baby to adopt? So we made the trip back to the airport to collect our second bundle. It was then that I met my daughter, a precious baby with the darkest brown eyes I'd ever seen. We named her Alex.

SOMETHING IS
VERY WRONG

B Y THE TIME LOUIS WAS three years of age, he'd become impossible to handle. He was extremely compulsive and would have severe temper tantrums all day long. I decided the time had come to make an appointment with a pediatric neurologist. While in the waiting room, I noticed a mother sitting beside me holding a baby girl about nine months old. The child was clearly mentally disabled.

Here I was, a young mother watching my son destroy the elegant waiting room. He ran around, grabbing whatever he could and throwing it on the floor. Just then, he noticed the sweet looking baby and began to play peek-a-boo. The more animated he got, the more she smiled. At that moment I was reminded that life is tough for everyone. Though I may have been at my wits' end with my son, at least he could walk and talk, something this baby girl might never experience. Maybe my son isn't perfect, and maybe he has problems, but he is my son, and I love him.

Louis was diagnosed with Pervasive Developmental Disorder, Attention Deficit Hyperactivity Disorder, and mild retardation. This was not exactly a shock to me.

As the years went on, Louis became significantly harder to handle. He was growing taller and becoming stronger. He would have these fits of rage, destroying everything around him. He was like a tornado, just demolishing everything and everyone in his path. He was expelled from every playgroup and school to which we sent him. Eventually, he got accepted to a special kids program in our local public school district. That gave us some respite, but the program only lasted a total of two hours a day. Did these administrators not realize that there are twenty-four hours in a day? Two hours with a kid that has special needs is hardly enough! He would be terrific for those two hours. The teachers and therapists loved him and reported no signs of dysfunction or aggressive behavior. What they didn't seem to realize was that he was like a boiling pot of water. He could hold it in for two hours, enjoying the one-on-one attention. As soon as he got home, his emotions exploded like a time-bomb. He just went mad. He would run around the house, hitting and kicking everything in sight with absolutely no control over what he was doing. The public school system would not help us since their rules only allowed involvement with problems observed in the school setting. Anything that was happening at home was not their problem.

As a mother, I was devastated, but I'd gotten my wish. I wanted a child. I took it for granted that he would be a healthy child. I didn't have the physical or emotional energy to deal with a child like him. There was no respite! I used to tell Nathaniel that five healthy kids would still be easier than one Louis. It was impossible to live a normal life. We couldn't go out anymore because he would make a scene and cause too much trouble, and we couldn't keep him in the house all day because he would go nuts. We had no idea how to handle this boy, and the worst thing about the whole situation was that he seemed to be getting progressively worse.

The older he got, the more frightening it became. The anger in his eyes scared the living daylights out of me. It was as if some scary monster had crept into my sweet boy's head and taken full control. He threw rocks at cars, and fought with everyone. It got so bad that one day, while fighting with a boy in the neighborhood, Louis began to choke him.

There is only so much that love and nurture can do for a

child. So much of who we are and what we do stems from our inborn nature. These things are almost impossible to change, it's in our DNA.

The downside of adopting foreign children is that unlike in the United States (where everything is documented), often you know nothing about the biological parents of these children. The father could be an axe-murderer and the mother a druggie. You just don't know. It is a toss-up and a risk that you take when you go the route of adoption. How could we have known that our Louis would inherit so many problems? How could anyone have known that the little baby we took into our home and hearts, would suffer from severe mental and psychological disorders?

Since he managed to do okay in school, the Board of Education refused to help us. He was seeing some of the best psychiatrists, and was taking several mood-stabilizing drugs, none of which seemed to be working. He needed to be placed in a safe environment where he would get all the help he needed, but this place eluded us.

One afternoon during one of Louis' usual fits of rage, he pushed me down. I fell backwards and hit the ground hard. He had never done that before. I was petrified, and afraid to get up. It was shocking that my Louis could actually hurt me, albeit unintentionally. Louis himself felt terrible, and started crying like a baby.

We couldn't postpone it any longer. Nathaniel came home, coaxed Louis into our car, and drove him to the nearest psychiatric ward for children. My heart was in pieces. My poor son, he doesn't mean it. He never means it. He wants to be good, but somehow his mental illness always takes over.

How can you stay angry at someone who has so little control over what he is doing?

In November of 2010, we learned about a new residential treatment home for kids that would meet all of our son's needs. It sounded perfect for Louis. He'd been in so many programs that were not right for him. He needed a very structured multi-disciplinary plan that would give him 24/7 supervision. After years of tormented searching, we'd finally found a proper home for our son. The counselors, therapists, and teachers all loved him and took great care of him. He flourished in his new environment.

When Louis turned eighteen, he began to hear "the voices." They would tell him to hurt himself and do very bad things. The voices made him crazy. He became paranoid and extremely depressed. He threatened to hurt himself over and over again. Louis admitted himself into one psychiatric hospital after the next, trying desperately to get help. Finally we found him a great psychiatric program that stabilized his medication, and the voices began to dissipate.

In the summer of 2017, he was diagnosed with schizophrenia. The facility he'd lived in for so many years was unable to accommodate his new needs. He was a young man now, no longer a child, with severe mental illness.

Thankfully, we soon found our son a wonderful residential home for adults, where he resides to this day. His schizophrenia is managed by strong anti-hallucinogenic drugs that help control the voices. But every so often, they come back to haunt him.

He currently attends a special needs high school and works at simple after-school jobs. He cuts grass, delivers pizza, and assists with the Volunteer Ambulance Corp. He recently opened his own fish and bait shop, which is very successful. Yes, the program has to hire someone to watch over him as he works, but he feels accomplished and happy. Don't get me wrong, he will always have these demons deep inside, but for now they are kept at bay. He feels happy, secure, and loved, which is what every mother wants for her child.

SHE IS JUST A TEENAGER

TEENAGERS COME DOWN TO EARTH to punish us for all the sins we've committed. You love them, but they aren't easy. They have their own language. And somehow they know how to push every single button that will drive us crazy. Anyone who has ever dealt with teenagers knows exactly what I am talking about. You start off with this adorable rosy-cheeked child. This little boy or girl charms your socks off with dimpled smiles and soft, complacent cooing. Then your child becomes mobile. That's when the real work begins. There is no need to go to the gym anymore. You are receiving a full cardio work-out every second of every day running after this kid. This impish-looking child will figure out the most dangerous thing to touch and the smallest roundest thing to stick in his or her mouth. You buy your child age-appropriate toys, but his favorite activity is to climb up onto the kitchen counter and pull at any electric cord he can find, which then of course goes into his mouth. When he gets bored, he decides to insert that wet, sticky cord into those cool little holes called sockets! You have to watch these adorable little toddlers every second of every day. Finally, your kid learns to fear danger and becomes a pleasure once again. But don't be fooled, young mothers and fathers! Don't let them fool you into thinking that this peaceful stage will last. If you are one of the lucky ones, you get a break for a few years and can actually enjoy some of life's moments with your child. But then when you aren't looking, something strange happens. Suddenly, the child who once thought you were the coolest and most wonderful parent on earth, now hates everything about you.

There are two reasons why most of us manage to survive

raising teens. First of all, they are our children. We can't just drop them off at the mall, and forget to pick them up for a few years. It doesn't work. Trust me, I've tried (just kidding). They all find their way back home somehow. We are sticking it out because our job is to guide them until their imminent return to the straight-and-narrow.

When we adopted our daughter Alex, we were given no background information about her birth parents. That may have prepared us somewhat for the rough waters that lay ahead.

When she was a toddler, I called her my cold fish. She would never want to hold my hand or be hugged or kissed. She was her own little person, and from day one she knew what she wanted. She was a determined and happy little girl. Nothing fazed her. Growing up with a brother like Louis made her strong and resilient. He would drive her crazy and she would fearlessly bop him on the head anytime she decided she'd had enough. As she got older she became increasingly popular. Her friends loved her. She was fun to be around and became a real leader.

When Alex turned eleven, things began to change. She started getting into trouble. Big trouble. First, she broke into my friend's house and destroyed everything. She took marshmallow fluff and glue and smeared it all over their computer keyboards. My friend was kind enough not to press charges, but understandably, never spoke to my daughter again. Alex continued stealing and doing poorly in school. Within two years' time, she went from being Miss Popular to not having a single friend by her side.

As she got older, her moods fluctuated constantly. One

minute she would be "manic" and the next she would be kicking and screaming on the floor like a two year old. I couldn't comprehend what was happening. Was it all normal pre-teen stuff? Deep down I knew it was not normal at all. Yet I held onto the belief that this would be a short-lived problem. Eventually, I had to admit that something was terribly wrong. We took Alex to top therapists, but her behavior did not improve.

She began skipping school and hanging out with the wrong crowd. She started acting and dressing differently. The amount of time she was spending on internet chat rooms seemed unsafe to us, so Nathaniel cancelled our internet service. But she would always find ways to circumvent any boundaries we set. She stole money from us, and went downtown. She purchased her own cell phone, and began communicating with boys who were way too old for her.

Defiant to the utmost, she would stay out all night, while we worried where she was. I could not keep anything valuable in the house. She stole my credit cards, phones, iPads, clothing — you name it, she stole it. If it wasn't nailed down to the floor, she took it. I would be sure that she was telling me the truth, only to find out later I'd been fooled once again.

The scariest part about my daughter was that she exhibited no remorse. She would do whatever she wanted, whenever she wanted, never expressing the slightest regret. She was always ready to do it again, without any apparent feelings of guilt. She didn't seem to have demonic voices telling her what to do. This angered me. So she was on the war path, and I became Target Enemy Number One. She knew how to manipulate her father. It was simple. All she had to do was throw a dramatic fit combined with copious tears, and within minutes he would buckle. I was different. I was the tough one. Needless to say, we often disagreed about how to deal with her, which made matters worse. He always felt bad for her, and I would not let her get away with everything. When I came down hard on Alex, Nathaniel would reprimand me, which sparked a screaming match between myself and Alex. She always won.

The harder we tried to keep her safe, the harder she would fight us and get herself in trouble. She finally got kicked out of school. Her moods worsened and we knew drugs were involved. This, too, was a bitter pill to swallow.

We'd given Alex the best childhood we could. We'd sent her to the best schools and camps, and always made sure she knew how much we loved her. Regarding her adoption, we were always open and honest. We told her that the day we were lucky enough to adopt her was one of the happiest days of our lives. I thought we did everything right. My goal was to be the best mother ever, yet I seemed to be failing miserably.

By fourteen, her behavior was so dangerous that we were in uncharted territory. We had the police on speed dial and Officer Thomas would always thank me for the brownies that I had ready for him during his nightly visits to our house. I am ashamed to say this but inside I almost *wanted* her to get into serious trouble and spend a night in jail. I figured that would teach her a lesson.

Thinking back, I really believe that so much of what she was dealing with could have been controlled if I could have disciplined her without being undermined. I was never allowed to punish her. When I tried, Nathaniel disagreed so it was never effective. Parents need to be on the same page, and we weren't even in the same chapter. She was clever, and used this to her advantage. I felt she was making a conscious decision not to behave. She was on a self-destructive path, a downhill spiral.

The sad truth was that Alex's issues, and our conflicting theories on how best to deal with them, were damaging our marriage, and disrupting the peace in our home.

One night, after punching the walls in a fit of rage, she came over to me and said in an eerily quiet voice, "Mother, one day I am going to kill you. You'll see, I am going to take a knife and slice your neck from side to side and I'll be happy watching the blood run down." It takes a lot to scare me but somehow, I believed her. For weeks I had nightmares of her trying to kill me in different ways. I even dreamed that she came up from behind me and tried to strangle me.

Nathaniel finally agreed that we needed to find her another place to live, where she would get the help she so desperately needed. We found a boarding school that catered to teens like my daughter. Their one and only rule was: NO drugs allowed on school grounds. Guess what? Alex was kicked out after just three weeks. She was caught using drugs front and center, in the school lobby.

Now what? After much research, we found a facility in Texas that had a great reputation for helping kids like this. I just hoped it would work. Once again, she refused to listen to the rules, and was constantly losing privileges due to inexcusable behavior. Even the best facilities in the country couldn't control my daughter. The whole situation was beyond depressing.

After six months of extensive therapy, they released her back into the real world, and she joined a family who lived within a few miles of the facility. Within two weeks' time she was sent packing. Currently, she is in Utah at a new treatment center, and we are hoping that this one helps here resolve some of her issues. We hope.

AN ANGEL IS BORN

A S OUR CHILDREN LOUIS AND Alex grew older, we decided to adopt again, but only from the United States! It would take over three years for us to find our daughter. First, we had to write a descriptive "bio" of ourselves and our family, explaining to each birth mother why she should choose us. There were hundreds of couples looking to adopt babies in the United States, so I had to be creative. I had to make ours stand out from the crowd and get the birth mother's attention, so I decided to have fun with it. After a month of my hard work, my special bio looked like a project that I would have brought home when I was in kindergarten. But I sent it anyway, since at least it showed vibrant creativity! Maybe the woman reading this would also see how hard I'd worked and feel bad for me. "This lady has too much time on her hands," she might think. "I'd better give her my kid, so she can do something productive with her life." I sent in my resume-mural and just prayed. I prayed that someone normal and nice would choose us.

After a year of waiting anxiously, the adoption agency called with good news. There was a woman in Nebraska who had chosen our resume. We were beaming with excitement and began to sink endless amounts of money into the adoption process, only to be told two months later that the birth mother had changed her mind. She decided to keep her baby. Now I had to start from scratch again, feeling intensely disappointed.

Within a few month's time, we were told by our agency that another mother had chosen us as well. Great! Knowing she could also change her mind, I was cautiously optimistic. The birth mother is generally given five to ten family bios for review and decides which family she would like to work with. I was extremely nervous. What if I wrote the wrong thing? Maybe she'd say, "There is no way I am giving my kid to these nuts." I didn't think I was nutty. But I don't think any nutty person thinks he or she is nutty. That's what makes them a nut in the first place.

Karen, a birth mother from Massachusetts chose us. We were the lucky winners. She wanted to meet us at a location close to her home. This was quite a drive for us but of course, we said, "No problem!" We were to meet at Cocoa's Coffee House. In the parking lot, I told Nathaniel that I was nervous. Maybe she had dormant psychological disorders that would be passed on to this unborn baby? What if we only learned of them when the baby turned two, like Louis?

We walked through the door of the coffee house. It smelled of old cigarettes and burnt toast. I looked around the room, and had no idea for whom I was searching. I'd forgotten to ask the birth mother what she looked like and what she'd be wearing. Within a minute, a woman with long brown hair and large round belly motioned for us to sit down. That was her! Our potential birth mother. We all sat down, introducing ourselves as though it was a business meeting.

Then we started talking. It was a sweet and simple conversation, and it went smoothly. Personally, I can make conversation with a tree stump and keep it going for some time. So in this situation, my talent helped tremendously. Karen was a pleasant woman who knew what she wanted. I just needed to make sure that she was emotionally healthy and stable. I didn't have an ounce of energy left to deal with another disturbed child.

Karen began her story. She had a six year old daughter from a previous marriage. After the relationship became abusive, she decided to leave. During this time she was told by her doctor that she would never conceive a child again due to complications during delivery. This news did not sadden her, she said, since she already had a beautiful daughter. A few years later, she began dating a man with whom she was now deeply in love. Six months into the relationship, she took a home pregnancy test that showed positive. After her doctor confirmed that she was indeed pregnant, he told her the baby was a miracle! Here she was with this "miracle baby" whom she loved, but felt she could not take care of. She could barely keep herself and her daughter afloat. How was she supposed to take care of another one? When her boyfriend found out, he panicked and left her. She still loved him. She just believed that he couldn't handle the responsibility of being a father.

She had just started a full-time job with benefits, and she needed to give all her love to her six-year old daughter. She'd made the tough but responsible decision to call an adoption agency and give her baby to a family who could be amazing parents to her unborn child.

During the whole conversation, I kept wondering: Does she like me? I just tried to make the best and most honest impression, and then it was her decision. As we left the coffee house, I gave her a big hug and promised her that if given the chance, we would always care for and love her child. That was it. Meeting adjourned. Now we would wait for her decision.

We didn't have to wait long. The next day the agency called us, happily relaying the news that Karen loved us. I was euphoric, but tried to keep in mind that the deal was far from done. I knew that numerous things could go wrong from then until the baby was born, and just hoped and prayed that we would have the chance to raise her little one as our own.

A few months went by. I talked to Karen quite often, and a real bond began to form between the two of us. One day, Karen called me telling me she was in labor. I would have loved to be in the delivery room with her to experience my baby being born, but she didn't give me that option. She made it very clear that she was going to do this her way. She wanted no one in the delivery room, and she wanted the first twenty-four hour period alone with her baby. This was the hardest part for me. I knew of so many cases where the birth mother changed her mind once she lay eyes on her baby. It becomes more real to her, and she can't go through with it. I knew if that happened, we would be heartbroken. You have very little control over anything in adoption. All the big decisions are made by your prospective birth mother, and that is very, very difficult. Those twenty-four hours felt like a lifetime. I was dying to see what the baby looked like, what she felt and smelled like. My potential baby was in a room down the hall, but I was not allowed to go near her. Those were the rules.

Thankfully, in the final hour, Karen gave her baby a loving kiss and said her good-byes. She wrote her baby a long letter telling her why she had to give her up and how she would love her until the end of time. I had the utmost respect for her at that moment. She was willing to give up her chance of motherhood to ensure that her child was raised well, with everything she needed.

It was then that I held my baby daughter Sarah for the very first time.

She was beautiful. She was content. She was a blonde, plump, pink bundle of joy. We fell in love right away! We love to do the surprise thing so, of course, we surprised my parents yet again. They thought we were out of our minds. They knew how much stress we were under concerning my health and our many issues with Louis and Alex. However, I didn't care what anyone thought. I was going to have my big family, and no one was going to tell me otherwise.

I was just so happy. She was so loving, even as a little baby. I called her my cuddle-bug. She was going to be my special girl and make me proud. I felt it. I knew it! I prayed for it.

Additionally, Nathaniel and I had recently opened a chain of second-hand clothing stores, which were doing very well. The success of our businesses was a blessing from God, and we acknowledged Him daily.

THE DISABLED IMMUNE SYSTEM

I WAS BUSY. I HAD two children in school, Baby Sarah at home, and was trying to manage my disease as best as I could. I think I was doing okay. Life was far from perfect, but I took it day by day.

During this period of time, I was still going to doctors who were off the-beaten-track, as well as surgeons who'd agreed to operate on any part of my body that became cancerous. Wherever I noticed a growing enlargement, I would tell the surgeon to remove it.

I don't think my body ever fully recovered after the bone marrow transplant, all those years ago. I don't know how any physical body could fully recover after so much toxic infusion and radiation.

My energy level was "eh". Sometimes I had a lot of energy, and sometimes I had no energy at all. The hardest part was that when I *had* energy, I didn't know how long it was going to last. Would it last for a day, a week, or a month? Getting tired was not like needing to take a nap. It was more like, if I don't get into bed right now, I'm gonna collapse on this floor. There were weeks where I was so weak, that I just couldn't get out of bed. It was difficult to deal with, especially while trying to reconstruct normalcy in my family life. Whatever germ was going around, I would get. When my kids started preschool, they became my walking petri dishes! They really wanted to share everything with their mom, especially their colds and sore throats.

I would frequent doctors once a month to have a basic check up. The amount of time I was actually seen by the doctor was never more than three to five minutes, tops. But with traveling and waiting time, it took up most of the day.

I understand if someone is running a little late, but who runs three hours late besides doctors? The better they are, the longer your wait time is going to be. If the doctor was just an average physician, you could expect a half hour wait. If the doctor had a semi-decent reputation, the wait time would be about an hour. But if your specialist was extra good at what he does, your minimum wait time would be in the two-hour range.

What nerve! Everyone in the waiting room complains, but they'll all wait three weeks in his waiting room to see him nonetheless. Some doctors' offices display a fancy coffee machine in the waiting room and expect you to be too grateful to complain. Oh, yeah, thanks for giving me a cup of coffee while I waste my whole day here waiting for the doctor. No, coffee is just not going to cut it. You know you are in trouble when you go into the waiting room with fifty patients sitting on couches watching the seventy-five foot television screen, figuring that it will help distract us from the fact that they are making us wait forever. I always wanted to go into my doctor's office and say, "You know, my time is just as valuable as yours. You owe me two hundred and fifty dollars for the two hours that I just spent sitting on your ugly couch, drinking your stale coffee and watching the boring house decorator channel. I've got a life, too, ya know."

Now there are always two waiting rooms, the big one that everyone gathers in and the "trick one" that makes you think you are going in to see the doctor. The staff is aware that a probable riot will form after the second hour wait time is up. So to avoid the anger of the masses, the nurses begin to bring patients into the second waiting room. Don't even think of getting into one of those paper tablecloths they have the gall to call a gown unless you want to freeze for another hour. Always make sure you have a warm pair of socks handy as well. They keep these places at Arctic temperature levels, so you'd better be prepared. The second waiting room is the worst, especially if you are coming to see the doctor and waiting for test results. It is beyond cruel. You know the doctor has your results, and that they are probably already in that colored folder with your name on it, but you still have to wait another hour until the doctor is ready to see you. It is just plain torture.

One doctor's waiting room in particular stands out in my mind, perhaps because my wait became worthwhile. Every so often I would find a magazine of interest. This doctor kept me waiting for over two hours. Most of those visits are a blur to me but this one time I remember quite clearly. I had picked up a medical journal with the title "New News For Couples With Infertility". That piqued my interest, so I began to read. The article explained how a lot of couples who were dealing with various infertility problems were choosing egg donors. What is egg donation? The whole idea was science-fiction to me. There are clinics that find women who, for one reason or another, are willing to sell their eggs. Many of these women are college students who are paying their way through school. They take hormone shots for some time to increase their number of eggs. After some time, the eggs are retrieved and utilized for various infertility treatments. When all is complete, the woman is paid anywhere from six to twelve thousand dollars.

So I began to inquire about this fascinating new world of

egg donation. I found a few reputable websites, and started working from there. I went to one website that had over five hundred egg donors to choose from. This was the first time in my life where the situation was reversed. I was in the driver's seat now. I was the one choosing and deciding, and it felt great. I mean, really great. I was asked to type in all kinds of information that would help filter choices down to a select few. For example: How tall? What ethnic background, age bracket and race? You name it, they asked it. It even went so far as to ask the egg donors how much school they'd completed and how well they'd done. It was unbelievable. So I began typing and started looking at the possible egg donors of interest. Some of the women were quite beautiful, but I knew that was not half as important as finding someone with a good heart. However, it was really hard to know just by seeing a photograph and lines of random information. Yes, it is great for me to know that you are an outdoorsy kind of person and you love cats, but how can I figure out if you have a good soul?

That was when I found a site called Reproductive Hearts. Not only did they screen their candidates extremely well, but each bio came with a three-minute video clip of the egg donor describing herself and what was important to her in life. Watching a video gave me a bit of insight into who the woman really was.

A few candidates who had seemed likable at first, were scratched off the list after I viewed their videos. After weeks of reviewing hundreds of bios, I finally had my top three choices. This game I was playing was fascinating. Today you can personalize anything. But this was not like personalizing a coffee mug or photo book. Here I was personalizing my own baby. That's pretty unbelievable stuff. I asked Nathaniel what he thought about my final three selections. I was choosing my hubby a concubine of sorts so I thought it was only fair to let him choose the lucky lady. He listened closely to all three videos and right away expressed a preference for "the lady behind door #2". Great minds think alike, since she was my first choice as well. We picked Lady #2, because she seemed so sweet and genuine, and that was exactly what we were looking for. We moved forward.

THE SHOCKING DIAGNOSIS

S ARAH HAD JUST TURNED ONE and we were enjoying her every day. As time went on, Nathaniel began complaining that he was not feeling well. He was losing weight and getting very weak. We figured his body was fighting some infection and we'd just have to wait it out. Within a matter of weeks, he became so weak that he could barely walk. We knew we had to get this checked out.

We made an appointment with a pulmonary specialist. After we'd collectively downed six cups of coffee and watched four news programs, the doctor was finally ready to see us. At the end of a thorough examination, the doctor advised us to return the following week, after receiving a chest X-ray and CT scan.

I remember Nathaniel telling the doctor that he felt like he was dying. I was shocked. I knew he was feeling horrible, but I hadn't realized how badly.

One week later, we waited in the "second" waiting room, both too afraid to talk. We just waited and waited. Out of the corner of my eye, I saw the doctor discussing something with one of his colleagues. They were pointing to that ominous light box with some poor guy's CT scan inside. My heart started to race. I started to panic. Oh, God, what happens if something is seriously wrong with my love? The possibility had never entered into my mind. **I** was the one who was sick. I was the one who was going through life with this stupid cancer thing inside me at all times.

Okay, I told myself, just relax, you're panicking for nothing. I tried to convince myself of that, but my heart would not stop racing. Then I thought I saw the two concerned looking doctors take a quick glance into our room. *Don't look into our little waiting room!* They were walking in. *Please don't walk in here! You look way too worried!*

Solemnly, they entered our room. They had the x-rays in their hands, and that look on their faces. I knew that look all too well. It was that awkward look they have when they are about to share unpleasant news with you. *Don't give me that look, please.*

The doctor carefully took the X-ray out and put it up in the light box of our little room. He began to explain that there were some disconcerting factors in Nathaniel's CT scan. Then they said those dreaded words: "Mr. Harot, your CT shows a large mass in your chest, which we think might be cancerous. We are so very sorry."

I was shocked. What do you mean he has cancer? You must be confused. **I** am the one with the big C word, not him! You must have gotten our slides confused. Nathaniel was as calm as a cucumber. Or perhaps he just didn't have the energy to panic. But I did. I asked the doctor how this could be. What were we going to do? Was it curable or treatable?

The next step was the biopsy. Even a simple little biopsy frightens the life out of most people. The hardest part of Nathaniel's biopsy was the location of the mass. It was near his heart which made the procedure all the more difficult. After an interminable three hour wait, the doctor called us back in with the results. The doctor, who already knew my whole history with Hodgkin's lymphoma began by telling us that the odds of spouses getting the same cancer at such young ages were one in a million. He told us we would have better odds at winning the lottery. Nathaniel was diagnosed with non-Hodgkins lymphoma, a slightly different form of lymphoma, but lymphoma nonetheless. It was not like we'd both been exposed to some kind of chemical that would have made us get sick with the same disease. I'd been diagnosed by the time I was twenty. I hadn't even met Nathaniel yet.

I couldn't believe this was happening.

Word quickly spread around our community, as this kind of news generally does. People were shocked that this was happening to us. Wasn't this just too much? They were right, it was too much. It felt unfair. Why couldn't I beat the odds by being the one in a million who won the lottery? Why did it always have to go the other way, the bad way, the hard way?

After a few days of my brain trying to process what had just happened, I got into my Go Mode. Okay, this is what God is testing us with, but He is good. We might have to struggle to get over this hurdle, but in the end, He was going to make it okay. How did I know? I just did.

I found out everything there was to know about non-Hodgkin's lymphoma. I read every article, looked up every new term, and armed myself with as much information as I could. Doctors could help, but I had lost faith in many of them over the years. I believed that you had to be your own advocate.

Whenever I went for surgery, I would take the surgeon's hand and tell him to please take good care of me.

"I know you do this all the time," I'd begin, "but there is only one me. Please take care of me like you would a member of your own family." I didn't want the surgeon thinking of me simply as a piece of meat, which is usually the case. I wanted to remind him that I was real, I was human! I was someone's wife, daughter, sister, and mother. Not just a one hundred-pound piece of beef.

By the time Nathaniel started his chemotherapy, he was extremely sick. It was amazing how fast it all happened. In a matter of weeks, he went from being a productive young man to a sick, incapacitated individual who could barely lift his head off the pillow. I was scared because he was losing strength so quickly. He was going downhill fast.

We were referred to a well-known lymphoma specialist by the name of Dr. Andre Boy. On our first visit, we were not prepared for the four-hour average wait time to see this doctor. Then he breezed into the room like a whirlwind. He was super-confident that Nathaniel would be okay. He was very reassuring, and seemed to be highly knowledgeable and competent. The best thing about Dr. Boy was his temperament. He was not an alarmist, which was exactly the kind of doctor we sought. The last thing I needed in my life was some doctor overreacting, and scaring us unnecessarily.

The doctor scheduled Nathaniel's first round of chemotherapy for the very next day. Having his intravenous chemotherapy drips as an outpatient made a world of difference.

Nathaniel had the typical side effects, such as hair loss and mouth sores, but within a week's time he started feeling better. The chemo agents killed more and more of his cancer cells every day.

Never in a million years did I imagine the tables would be turned, but I was with him every step of the way. My

Nathaniel was the patient, and I the caretaker. Life throws you curve balls, and this was definitely a biggie for us.

After six months of treatment, the only thing left for Nathaniel to do was to finish up his month of radiation. That was the hardest part for him. I'd had a lot of radiation over the years, but although weak, I'd never experienced much pain while undergoing those treatments.

Nathaniel's skin began to burn badly. He was in a lot of pain. It was very hard for me to see him suffer, but I knew we were nearing the end of this phase. I prayed to God, as I always did, that his scan would come back negative. It did. He would need to go for more scans after three months, then six months, and one more at the end of the year. Finally, Nathaniel was in remission.

I never took for granted all the blessings that God has bestowed upon me throughout my life. Yes, I had a lot of health-related problems but in between the raindrops, I was living a fairly good life. I was happily married to my best friend, and had a growing family. I had loving parents who would turn over the world for me, and a brother who was there for me no matter what. And although the two older children kept us on our toes, they also brought many smiles. I could fill a book with the hilarious remarks my kids said during their formative years.

Nathaniel and I traveled as much as we could, and always got into some kind of trouble. We had a funny story that went along with everything we did. God had given me many tests but he also gave me the resources to get through it all and still be able to smile happily. To this day, I love everything about life, I love nature and animals. I love photography and travel. I love to cook, and even more, I love to eat! My life was filled with endless blessings that I appreciated deeply. There were thousands of great days, filled with love, fun, and happiness.

THE TOASTER OVEN

ONWARD, AND MARCH. WE HAD three children, but I would have given anything to experience the miracle of a child growing inside of me. Nathaniel was nervous. He didn't think that my body could handle the stresses of pregnancy. Reluctantly, I agreed with him. I was still dealing with my cancer, and my body had gone through so much already. I wanted another child very much. Perhaps someone else could carry it for me?

I needed a personal toaster oven to cook my baby to perfection, but where would I find one? I didn't think my local Walmart would be carrying this kind of toaster. I spoke to my infertility doctor, and he told me about surrogate pregnancies. There are women willing to "lend" their uterus for a mere $25,000. These women are called gestational carriers. Most are married women who already have children and need the money. It is not as simple as the egg donor's job. This woman really has to commit to this process. So this was my next mission. I needed to find the right oven, but I had no idea where I would find someone who could fill the position.

The infertility clinic helped me with my search, and after a few months, we found our guardian angel. Tara was divorced with two kids. She loved being pregnant, but was done having her own kids. She always wanted to help a couple in need, and the money would be helpful as well. We met, and it was love at first. I had never in my life met someone like Tara. She had a heart of gold and wanted nothing but to make sure that she would be able to grant us our own biological child. Okay, our own 50% biological child, but that was as good as it was going to get. Don't get me wrong; I still dreamed that maybe one day I would bear my own biological child. However, whether it was fair or not, I knew the chances were low. I guess it was just not destined to be. I had to come to terms with that realization. It was not easy. I don't think I've ever fully come to terms with it. I just learned to avoid thinking about it and thank God for what I did have, which was a lot.

Everything was in place. The clinic was able to extract thirty viable embryos from our egg donor. Six embryos survived to the end. That meant six potential babies! Now Tara, our gestational carrier had to get more involved. She started taking hormone shots daily to prepare her uterus for the implantation of the embryos. We had all decided that we were comfortable putting two embryos in Tara's uterus. We were ready.

The big day came. If it worked, amazing, and if not, at least we tried. I called the doctor the morning of the transfer, and told him that I had a very strange favor to ask of him.

"Please say a quiet prayer before you begin the transfer," I begged him. "Ask God to make sure this baby will be healthy and well".

"Of course I will," he answered, moved. "I will pray for you, and I will pray for your embryos."

We decided on transferring two embryos in the hope that one of them would survive. After the transplant was done, the doctor called us and said everything looked good. We would now wait to find out if any of the embryos "took". In nine days, Tara would take a blood test that would reveal if she was pregnant or not.

It was a Friday morning when I got the call from the doctor. He sounded happy, and said he was thrilled to tell me that both embryos "took". I couldn't believe what was happening! I was hoping to have one baby, and now I was going to have …TWINS! Never, in my wildest dreams, did I imagine I would have twins. I didn't stop smiling for weeks on end. People may have thought I was finally going off the deep end, but I just couldn't help it. I was on cloud nine.

When Tara entered her eleventh week of pregnancy, she called me, hysterical. I could not calm her down, and I had no idea what had happened, but the more she cried, the more nervous I got. She told me that she'd just received her ultrasound results, and was told that one of the embryos had split in two. That meant that she was now carrying triplets (one set of identical twins and one set of fraternal twins).

She lost it. She said, "I can't give birth to three babies. I just can't do this."

I didn't know what to do. We met Tara in the city a few days later, at one of the top high-risk obstetrician's offices. We were told that the odds were highly against something like this happening. This doctor didn't know who we were, and had no idea that Weird Odds was our middle name.

He explained that carrying the pregnancy to term was too dangerous for Tara as well, as for our three babies. Serious decisions would need to be made.

We met Tara two weeks later, for her follow-up ultrasound which would clarify the status of our babies. On this screen, I witnessed all three babies with their three sets of fingers and toes. I heard the little heartbeats of my beautiful babies. Nathaniel and I were mesmerized. Teary-eyed, I marveled at how the triplets shared their cramped space so peacefully. Who had the heart to disturb their little world of oblivion and bliss?

It was devastating, but the doctor said he had no choice.

Two out of three lives had to be "terminated". There were Babies A, B, and C. Baby A kind of did his own thing. Baby B was the troublemaker who had split into Babies B and C. The doctor advised us to "dispose" of Babies B and C. Baby A had the best chance of surviving and being healthy. The next day, the doctor injected a poisonous dye into two little hearts, still beating strong. I was devastated.

I tried getting sympathy from Nathaniel, but it was not forthcoming. This is when the Men Are From Mars Women Are From Venus rule applies. Nathaniel said, "What's the big deal? We wanted a baby, so hopefully we're gonna have a baby."

I could not understand how the killing of two of our babies hadn't affected him in the least. But I did agree with him on this: I had to think of Baby A now. I had to make sure that my baby got through the next seven months, safe and snug as a bug in a rug.

CANCER, CANCER, GO AWAY!

DURING THE NEXT FEW MONTHS, as Tara's belly grew, the masses in my chest did the same. I knew I had to do something about my cancer, but I was afraid of what that would entail. I started getting a very bad infection from the synthetic mesh that had been inserted into my sternum years earlier. My skin, which was in poor condition from all the radiation began to get infected as well.

I was going to need a radical surgery. The infections were getting so bad that I was beginning to feel sick all the time. I had flu-like symptoms with fever and chills. I so wanted to be happy at this expectant time in my life, but this cancer thing just wouldn't give me a break. It was ruthless.

My idea of localized surgeries and vitamin drips had bought me a decade, but now I needed a different way to kill them off. The large cancerous masses in my chest and skin had to be removed, after which I would need to find a new weapon of destruction.

Dr. Boy recommended two extensive surgeries, both of which involved removing all affected tissue. The surgeon would then graft healthy skin (the size of a grapefruit) from my stomach to replace the removed skin. I think they called it a flap. It was a risky surgery but it had to be done. I literally felt like one of those Mr. Potato Heads that I used to love to play with when I was a kid. I would put the arm where the belly was supposed to go and the leg where the eye should have been. That is kind of what they did to me. They had to take me apart and try to put me back together again, like Humpty Dumpty.

When I awoke from the surgery, I was in terrible pain. It took me many weeks to recover from these surgeries, until

I felt well enough to go home. Finally, the first phase of my healing was over.

I knew what the second phase would be like. I was not ready to deal with the fact that I might actually have to go for more chemotherapy, and maybe even another bone marrow transplant. It was overwhelming. I was so weak. My body had to heal, and I had to be emotionally ready to proceed.

For years, Dr. Boy would hit me over the head with his newspaper and tell me that I should go for another bone marrow transplant. "It's a no-brainer!" he would say. I finally relented.

Siblings have a 25% chance of being a perfect match. I didn't have numerous brothers and sisters. I never minded growing up with just one brother. I'd always been happy with just him. I didn't think I needed more siblings, but now it would have helped! With one sibling, I only had a one in four chance of a match.

God was on my side, and the blood tests confirmed that my brother Jacob was a perfect match. So now I had a good donor, but what did that matter? My first transplant (where they infused me with my own preserved marrow) hadn't worked. So why would my brother's work any better? Dr. Boy explained to me that my body didn't "know" which cells were healthy and which were cancerous. My whole immune system was messed up.

Apparently, everyone is born with some cancer cells. A normal average body contains thousands of cancer cells. So why do some people get cancer and others don't? Because bodies that are wired correctly target the cells that don't look normal. The body sees these cells as a threat, and destroys them before they can mass produce. A person who gets cancer has an impaired immune system which does not recognize the danger of these cells, thereby allowing them to proliferate. Healthy marrow would destroy my enemy cells right away. That is how Dr. Boy explained it, and it made a lot of sense to me.

As I waited patiently for my body to heal, I was also waiting for my unborn child to arrive. The anticipation was real, but my mood was bittersweet, because I was in constant pain. I wanted to be joyous about my baby being born, yet I knew that within a few months of the baby's birth, I might be fighting for my life once again. **I could never just relax.** My disease overshadowed every part of my life, and I hated that.

On October 26,2010 Nathaniel and I grabbed our pre-packed bag, and headed to the hospital. Tara was in labor! By the time we got to the hospital, she had delivered a healthy baby boy. We were euphoric!

We named our son Sam after my grandfather, to whom I was extremely attached as a child. Sam was a star from the moment he was born. He had the sweetest little face and the smallest fingers and toes I'd ever seen. He was perfect, and he was all ours! My joy was indescribable. I never thought anyone could love someone else as much as I loved this newborn baby. And we'd only just met!

Sam was basically healthy, except for a minor kidney problem which eventually required surgery. He would need to be monitored in the ICU for a few weeks. The hospital was a five hour drive from where we lived: a difficult commute. Every day, I would sit by his crib and hold his little hand. He looked so distressed. It was painful to observe the nurses constantly poking him for blood. Meanwhile, the hospital had allowed us to live in a small room on the 6th floor until we were ready to take our son home. Still recovering from my surgeries, I had a catheter, as well as large wounds, that needed to be cleaned and sterilized three times a day. I was also receiving antibiotics intravenously.

It was not easy doing all this in a tiny little hospital room the size of a closet but we did it. We'd become world-class jugglers. Four weeks later, we drove home with our little boy.

THE TRANSPLANT
- THE SEQUEL

WHEN SAM WAS FIVE MONTHS old, it was time to proceed with my health itinerary once again. Dr. Boy did not mince words. A second bone marrow transplant was imperative; I had no choice. I thought I would never agree to chemotherapy again, but I had four children who depended on me now. I had to do everything in my power to get completely healthy, once and for all.

A body has to be in decent condition to survive a transplant. I was still young, and a good candidate, but I had a new baby at home! I wanted to spend every waking minute with my miracle bundle of joy. If I were to proceed with the transplant now, it would mean leaving all of my children for almost two full months! Missing out on two months of a baby's life is missing out on a lot. Everything happens so fast at that age. Little Sam would be doing all those cute and joyful things without a mother to clap gleefully with pride.

I didn't want to lose one minute of that. But of course, as usual, I had no choice. I had to think long term. If I wanted to be a mom to my beautiful children for many years to come, I would have to sacrifice the next two months.

The only good thing, and I mean really the ONLY good thing about being hospitalized for a bone marrow transplant is the "executive suite". Because your immune system levels drop so drastically, you are given a private room adjacent to the nurses' station.

In the winter of 2011, I entered my room on the tenth floor at St. Charles Hospital, the transplant floor. I was such an expert at being a hospital patient by now. I didn't bother bringing any personal pictures. I headed to the hospital with seven pairs of monkey PJ's, my smartphone, a book of Psalms, and of course my little black bag of goodies. I was scared, but I wanted desperately to be rid of this dreadful disease, once and for all.

We began with daily intravenous chemotherapy drips. I remember being nauseous, but not as horribly as the first time around almost twenty years ago. The anti-nausea drugs were considerably more effective. The chemo was then increased, and I became significantly weaker.

Anyone entering my room had to don a gown, mask, and gloves. The entire room had to be perfectly sterile at all times, due to my fragile physical state. Whoever was lucky enough to be on night shift with me had to sleep in the gown, mask, booties, and gloves. It seemed a bit ridiculous, but it was the only way. Did you ever actually try to breathe in one of those blue masks? It is quite uncomfortable for any length of time. First of all, you are inhaling your own old air, repeatedly. Even if you brushed your teeth that morning, trust me, your breath ain't perfect, and you are going to notice that right from the start. Then you get sweaty and tired, and the elastic on the back of the mask begins to give you a massive headache. Still, no one could enter my room without following strict protocol, no matter how uncomfortable. It was mandatory for my safety.

Also imperative was that no matter how ill I felt, I was to get out of bed every day and exercise. That was the last thing I wanted to do! I was tired from just breathing, and they wanted me to exercise? They had to be kidding, right? But they weren't joking around. The doctors would stress that an immobile body invites infection. If I didn't get up and get my heart pumping, I could end up with pneumonia, which in my case could be fatal. So I had no choice but to don a fresh pair of PJ's, unplug my IV pole, and venture outside my room. Since I was not allowed off the transplant floor, my exercise routine was walking around the nurses' stations repeatedly. I'd hang on to my IV pole for dear life, so it didn't go flying every time I turned a corner.

There was a walking chart in front of the nurses' station. Once around the floor was called a lap. You would put your room number down, and "log" how many laps you walked that day. At the end of the week, there would be a winner. I won every single week. I would just go round and round and round. I would go around twenty times per morning, and repeat the routine several times daily (depending on my level of wellness on that particular day).

I was fast, too. My father would often walk with me, and I would inevitably hurtle into everything in my path. My IV pole always had one wheel that inevitably veered to the right. It was like one of those shopping carts you get stuck with at the food store, that bumps around and veers you off course. Dad said I was a terrible driver, and that if there were any cops hiding in the corners, I would have had my pole confiscated long ago. He would put up signs in the hallway saying, "Patients beware, crazy driver coming through!" He was funny and always made me laugh. **Smiling and laughing have unbelievable healing powers.** When you are happy, your body naturally fares better. It is like a Jumbo-size energy drink for your immune system.

My father would be there as much as he could, but he and everyone else had busy lives. So it was lonely too, and Nathaniel and I had precious little time together. I didn't mind being alone in the room when I was feeling ill; then I just wanted to rest in bed, alone.

When I felt better, however, it became quite boring. You would think this hospital ward might have classes or activities for recovering patients. Apparently, most patients on the tenth floor are too sick to think about doing any activities, so there was no program whatsoever. For me, however, keeping busy was an integral part of my recovery.

One day, during lap number fifty-two around the ward, I came upon a real treasure. One of the doors to a usually locked closet was open. I peeked inside, and found an array of art supplies. I was ecstatic! I ran as fast as you can run with a stupid IV pole. Okay, I walked quickly to the nurses' station. I asked if I could perhaps borrow a few items from the supply closet, and they said yes! That was the founding moment of my home-made greeting cards. I began creating cards for everyone I loved. I made cards for my kids, for Nathaniel, and for my parents.

Every day I would try new ideas, and my creativity thrived. The cards were my lifeline. I had no patience to read and wasn't feeling well enough for conversation. Creating and designing cards was very peaceful for me. It helped me get my mind off of my problems by focusing only on the simple, relaxing task at hand. This activity kept me sane for three weeks.

Nathaniel would bring Sarah to visit me once a week. Since children were not allowed in my room at all, I had to meet my kids in a separate room, designed exclusively for family get-togethers. Alex, my oldest daughter rarely came. She complained that she couldn't stand the smell of hospitals.

Louis was already in his group home, and I think it would have been too much for him to see his mother in this state. Sam was an infant, so that left my Sarah.

Sarah always greeted me with a big smile and huge hug. One of the few positive memories I have of this time period were my special visits with Sarah. She wasn't scared, and didn't mind asking me a bunch of questions that I never minded answering. She was my angel. She had a heart of gold, and I was so very proud of her. I've always worked very hard on my children being respectful and kind to others, and she was my prodigy.

The most fearful day of my hospital stay, by far, was the day I started a new regimen of chemo agents. Suddenly, out of nowhere ten nurses and technicians invaded my tiny hospital room. They began frantically taking my blood pressure and checking my heart. I hadn't felt any different and I had no idea what was going on. Then the "heart zapper" machine appeared. You know, the one you've seen on TV episodes? Why was there a zapper machine in my room? Was I about to be zapped? I didn't want to be zapped.

An hour later, things had calmed down a bit, and most of the nurses had left my room. Dr. Boy finally arrived and explained that I'd just had congestive heart failure. My heart rate had dropped drastically, so the technicians were standing by to "jumpstart" me as soon as necessary. I hadn't sensed it at all. Thus began a series of heart tests - EKG's and echocardiograms. The test results showed my ejection fracture (which means how well my heart was pumping) was very weak.

This last chemo agent had weakened my heart. I'd

never had anything wrong with my heart before. The only thing I always had to worry about was my cancer. My heart was strong and had survived chemo treatments, a bone marrow transplant, radiation, and countless surgical procedures. This new chemo was breaking my heart, literally. I needed my heart! It wasn't like breaking a finger where I had other fingers to compensate. **I only have one heart and it has to last me a lifetime.** How could they have been so careless?

The next day, a cardiologist came into my room and handed me a pamphlet. It was about a machine they would be implanting in my heart. Not exactly casual reading!

Wait, it gets better. Not only would I have a device implanted in my body, but this machine is accompanied by a heart detector, worn around the waist in a fanny pack that I'd now have to carry around with me for the rest of my life. It picks up signals from the implanted device in your heart, and if the heart ever stops beating, it zaps it back into beating again. It was actually a portable baby zapper machine. NO WAY! No flipping way was I going to wear this fanny pack forever. First of all, I don't do fanny packs! Perhaps I might have considered it, had they put it into a Chanel or Hermes case. I also didn't want to have to carry something around that would remind me every minute of every day that I have this problem.

I was very upset about the whole thing. That is when Dr. Boy came in. I repeated to him what the cardiologist had said, and guess what he did? He hit me over the head with his newspaper and told me to forget about it.

"You are not going to need it." That is all he had to say. Whether it was true or not, I felt so much better.

A few months after the transplant, I went for a follow-up echo, and it showed that my heart was stronger and approaching normal levels again. I was more relieved than words can describe. I would need to take heart medication for the rest of my life (and follow up with a cardiologist three times a year), but I was okay with that.

A few weeks later, I received my brother's bone marrow, and almost instantly began to feel better. My blood counts slowly rose, and multiple anti-rejection drugs were prescribed. After two months of intense therapy, the doctors declared that I was ready to head home.

Dear reader, as soon as you're done reading my book, kindly march yourself over to your local hospital and tell them you want to be a transplant donor. They will swab the inside of your cheek once, and you are done. That is it. The screening used to involve having blood drawn, but now it is a three-second cheek swab, which will be registered in the international transplant bank. If someone is ever in need of a bone marrow transplant, and you are a match, you would only have to give up two hours of your day to give some blood, and voila! You just saved a life.

MEDICAL
BREAKTHROUGH

THREE MONTHS HAD PASSED, AND I was scheduled for my first PET scan since the transplant. I was pretty sure I was fine, but still quite nervous. How could I not be? The scan came back negative. Home free?

Two months later, the doctors did a repeat scan. This time the doctors reported that the transplant had **not** done the trick. Something new was growing. I couldn't believe it.

For the first time since my initial diagnosis, I fell into a deep depression which lasted over five months. I just wanted to go to sleep and never wake up. It was one of the worst feelings I have ever felt in my life. I sought out many doctors, until I finally found one who prescribed an antidepressant that really helped me get through this period of time. Up until now, as long as I had my family by my side, I was happy and able to cope. I honestly and wholeheartedly believed, all along, that everything would eventually be ok. But this was too much. Would it ever end?

A month later I received a package. It was a colossal box, wrapped in gold-glittered ribbon that shone like the sun. God had sent me a present. A present that I had been patiently awaiting for two decades. There was a card attached. It read:

To my dear Emma,

You have earned your wings by displaying tremendous faith and belief in me. Take this as a token of love and appreciation. I will always love you.

Love always, GOD.

Allow me to explain.

Dr. Boy told me that in his twenty-five years of treating Hodgkins patients, there had not been a real medical breakthrough in its treatment. Since the disease had such high rates of survival, not much funding was allocated to finding a cure. He proceeded to tell me that just last week, a new drug called Rituximab had been approved by the FDA, for patients with Hodgkin's lymphoma. Still in its experimental phase, this drug supposedly had a very high success rate. The only side effect of note, was some mild weakness. I could deal with that, but would it help?

Dr. Boy encouraged me to start taking it right away, and I did. One night after my shower, all my newly grown-in hair started to fall out in clumps. I'd gone through this so many times, I'd lost count. But I wasn't expecting it now. Tearfully, I asked the doctor what happened. Dr. Boy's response was that while this new medicine possessed some properties of chemo, it didn't destroy as many good cells. He reiterated that it was part of a targeted therapy program and that he'd never seen hair loss in any of his patients before. He admitted that he was aware of a few rare cases where hair loss had occurred. Of course, I was one of the rare few.

I felt like a Martian again, with soft fuzz on the top of my head, but this time I didn't mind. I had high hopes for this new drug. Hair was just…hair. Not wanting to frighten my young children, I kept my head covered day and night. I didn't want them to see their mother looking scary. I wanted to retain the image of a happy, fun, cool-looking mom that they'd always known.

The plan was for me to be given Rituximab intravenously every two weeks for one year's time. After six months of this new targeted therapy, I was scheduled for yet another PET scan.

The first time I was sent for one, I'd assumed it had something to do with either dogs or cats-what an odd name! It is similar to a CT scan, but much more thorough from a cancer perspective. At first, the nurse injected me with a radioactive dye. After the scan was over, I was literally radioactive. I had to stay away from anyone in the human race for the first few hours. The radioactive dye attaches itself to any cancer cells in the body and will light up if any cancer is found. I prayed the results would be normal, and my scan would appear black as night.

After completing the PET scan, I arrived at Dr. Boy's office and sat in his waiting room for over three hours. I used this time to pray and make little deals with God. My blood pressure was probably 300/300. Finally the doctor called me in to tell me the good news.

"Your scan is negative, and it looks good," he told me.

I couldn't believe it. That was the best thing anyone had told me in a long time. I was in such a state of extreme relief that I didn't know what to do with myself. I almost knocked him down with the biggest hug I had ever given to anyone. I felt so blessed and so taken care of by the One above. He had been watching over me and made sure I was okay. **This was my present wrapped in gold.**

Understandably, after all of the above, I felt a strong need to get away. Away from doctors, nurses, pills, IV pumps and everything else cancer-related. I decided that I would head to the Caribbean for a few days by myself. I would have loved to travel with Nathaniel, but he hates everything about those kinds of trips, especially the sun, sand, heat, and water-which is what the Caribbean is all about. It would be my own little escape, and I felt I deserved it.

Somehow, whenever I traveled alone, I manage to get into some kind of trouble. I have no idea why. I like to be adventurous and it tends to get me into a pickle quite often. During this particular trip, on the plane heading to the beautiful aquamarine waters of the Caribbean Islands, I was thoroughly engrossed in the flight movie. It was based on a true story, about a couple who'd traveled to one of the world's top diving sites. The captain had miscalculated and assumed everyone was back on board. To make a long story short, the couple was left out in the ocean and ended up getting eaten by hungry sharks. Why the airline would show a movie like that when we were all heading to the beach is beyond me. Maybe it was some sick joke the pilot decided to play on his passengers that day. All I can tell you is that it scared the living daylights out of me, but it made the three-hour flight fly by, literally!

During my second morning on the island, I decided to sign up for a snorkeling tour with the stingrays. This was arranged through the hotel, so safety was ensured. The boat took us out, mid-afternoon. It took about thirty minutes by speed-boat to reach our destination, an area which was absolutely breathtaking. The water was this perfect shade of blue/green, and we were virtually in the middle of the ocean, no land in sight. The water, however, was relatively shallow, no more than ten feet deep.

I donned my mask and jumped into the refreshingly cool,

clear water. In an instant, I found myself surrounded by giant sting-rays. Panicking, I lifted my head above the water. I just couldn't believe that these beautiful sea creatures weren't afraid of me. Eventually, I became more comfortable with my new marine friends, and began to swim alongside them. The beautiful sun-kissed waters, the sounds of the waves, and the serene ocean setting provided imagery I can still conjure up today when I need to de-stress.

The captain told us that we had an hour and a half of snorkel time, before heading back to the boat. I figured that would give me plenty of time to enjoy swimming in the water with my new aquatic buddies. I began following a baby stingray and its mother. In my entranced state, I didn't hear the whistle. My ears and eyes were mesmerized by what was going on all around me.

When I finally did lift my head out of the water, I found that I was nowhere near my boat. There were many boats in the water at the time, and I had no idea which one was mine. Help! I had all my personal belongings on the boat, including my clothing, my camera, my money, and-oh no, my passport! I had to find my boat. I tried to think of what my boat looked like, but for the life of me, I couldn't remember. I didn't think I would have to remember. We were the first boat out there, and I didn't know there would be other boats anchoring as well. They all looked the same to me, and I didn't recognize any of the people. I began to panic in earnest.

One by one, each boat would collect its passengers and be off. They were all leaving! What was I supposed to do? Should I just get on any boat and pray that I'd find my passport and other belongings once ashore? What if these boats weren't even heading towards the same beach? Finally, there was only one boat left but it was not mine. I asked the captain if I could please come aboard explaining to him that my boat had left without me, but he didn't want to take me.

Thinking back, I should have said, "I am getting on your stupid boat, whether you like it or not." I was in such an alarmed state that I wasn't thinking clearly. He told me that he had to return his passengers, but he would be back in about an hour. If I was still in the water, I should wave my hands up and down, and he would pick me up. Are you serious? Are you really going to leave me here in the middle of the ocean by myself?

That is exactly what he did. He left!

All alone, I recalled that terrible movie about the couple eaten by sharks. Now, I was really scared. Had I survived cancer, only to be inhaled by sharks for their 2:00 p.m. snack?

After what felt like hours of waiting, I noticed a boat coming towards me. It looked like a speck of dust from my vantage point, but it loomed larger as it approached. It was my boat and my captain. They'd come back to get me! When I got back on board, I realized what had probably saved me that day. On the way to our destination, I was conversing with two very sweet women from Canada. The captain informed me that these two women remembered "a woman from New York" whom they had not seen aboard when they arrived back to shore. Right away, they notified the captain, who quickly turned the boat around to get me. Thank God! Once again, I was saved. Okay, so that was not the best trip in the world, and it definitely did not give me the lasting peace and serenity I so craved, but I was safe and alive. I was grateful, and more than ready to return home.

THE ULTIMATE TEST

FOR THE FIRST TIME IN twenty years, I began to feel a mild sense of peace and tranquility. My daughters were in school, Louis was happy in his residential placement, and my toddler, Sam, was home with me.

My parents became those "snowbirds," the seniors who can't handle the cold New York weather and move down to Florida for half a year. My dad was still working and did not want to retire. He was and still is, a principal in the New York City Board of Education School System. He loved his job, and he was good at it. So he would stay in New York and work, while my mother would head down to the Sunshine State, playing her poolside mah-jong every Monday and Wednesday afternoon. Their marriage was never better. I guess absence makes the heart grow fonder!

But after two months of Florida, my mother could not bear another day without seeing her precious Sarah and Sam. She ate, slept, and breathed them. She lived for them. Her famous words were, "If anything ever happened to my Sam, I would kill myself!" She said it and she meant it. I knew this was not a normal thing for a grandmother to say, but she repeated it nevertheless. My otherwise-frugal mother was willing to pay an exorbitant amount of money to get on a flight to New York so she could see her grandkids. She would often say to me, "Are you kidding me? We don't love you. We had you just so one day we'd get grandkids." Ahh, so I was just a means to an end.

Life was good. Life was normal. For about ten-seconds.

My mother spent a week with us, enjoying every minute she could with her prince and princess. She'd started teaching Sarah how to knit, and spent hours a day on the living room floor playing games with Sam. Her flight was headed back to Florida on Tuesday morning, the same day Sam went to his "Terrific Toddler Music Class". He loved music, and was excited to go every week. For some inexplicable reason, on this particular day he was throwing a fit. He just didn't want to go. But of course, I convinced him that he would have fun as usual, and he went with a smile.

The date was February 13, 2012, a day that I will remember for the rest of my life. It was 10:30 a.m. when I got **the call**. It was Nathaniel. I immediately asked him where he was, because he was supposed to have taken my mother to the airport a half hour before.

"There's been an accident," he said numbly.

He was now in an ambulance with Sam heading to the emergency room. My mind started to race. I asked him if Sam was okay. I just wanted him to say yes.

In that same emotionless voice, he replied, "I don't know if he is going to be okay. It's bad, Emma. Very bad."

I don't even know what he said after that. I know that he was talking, but I didn't hear one word. An animalistic scream from the depths of my soul escaped my lips, and I just kept on screaming until my mother came running up the stairs.

"What happened?" she shrieked. "Did anything happen to my Sam? Please tell me that nothing happened to my Sam!"

I told her that there had been some kind of accident, but that's all I knew at the moment. Finally, I called Nathaniel back. He told me that an elderly man had been driving his car down the street, suffered a heart attack, and collapsed at the wheel. The unmanned car then sped down the street, jumped a curb, crossed three lawns, and finally stopped by crashing into a van-the van near which my Sam had been standing. My poor child was pinned helplessly between the van and the car...

Sam had been waiting patiently to be put into his car seat in the van. It was parked right beside the home's front door, which was a distance from the street. His teacher, Brenda, watched horrified as this unfolded in a matter of seconds. Before she could act, the car had already jumped the curb.

Poor Sam was only two years old. Some of the other children had fled out of harm's way seconds earlier, but he never saw it coming. It was like a missile aimed for his head. Why my Sam? Why was this happening to me? This could not be happening. It just couldn't be.

Brenda lifted my son into her arms, frantically calling out for help. People streamed out of their houses to find out what was going on. Within seconds, someone called an ambulance. The EMT took one look at Sam, and told Brenda that they were not equipped to transport someone so severely injured. A few minutes later, another ambulance arrived, gently took Sam from Brenda, with plans to race towards the nearest hospital. One of the neighbors contacted Nathaniel, who arrived on the scene just as the ambulance was closing its doors. He jumped into the back of the ambulance, then phoned me saying he would call me back as soon as they arrived at the emergency room.

My mother was now questioning me like a broken record. "What did he say? What happened?" she kept repeating.

I had already told her everything I knew, but she needed

more, and I understood. She needed to know that Sam was going to be okay, and I didn't know the answer to that yet.

All I knew was, I'd woken up a few hours ago, and sent my two-year-old cutie pie off to his music class. What happened next, I simply could not wrap my head around. The phones were ringing off the hook, people were coming in and out of my home, and I just sat there on the floor, disoriented, and not knowing what to do.

Slowly, my instincts returned to me, and I grabbed a book of Psalms and began reciting the verses. Please God protect me, shield me from evil. The verses expressed exactly what I wanted to say. At times, I suddenly cried out in deep anguish, "God Almighty, help me, help me get through this. Don't take my Sam away from me, Not my miracle baby!" I pleaded over and over again.

Nathaniel was calling. I picked up quickly, and asked him what was going on. He told me they'd rushed Sam into the operating room. Nathaniel was now in the waiting room, anxiously hoping for comforting news. The doctors had promised to do everything in their power to save our little boy.

I don't even remember how I got to the hospital that day. I just remember going up the elevator towards the children's ICU thinking, "I don't think I can handle this. I don't think I am strong enough for this." By that time, I knew that my Sam had survived the initial trauma and was now in an induced coma. The car's strong impact had fractured his little skull. Sam was in critical condition.

Nathaniel asked me if I was ready to see Sam and I said

yes. However, nothing could have prepared me for what I saw next.

The boy in the bed didn't resemble Sam at all. I looked at the unfamiliar creature before me, and burst into tears of sorrow and unbearable pain. How could this broken, doll-like figure be my Sam? He was attached to multiple machines by a mass of wires. His head was covered in white bandages as he lay there, still, with his eyes swollen shut. Tubes were hanging from everywhere. It was the saddest thing I had ever seen in my entire life. I had no idea how I was still standing on my own two feet, how my heart was still beating, and how I could even breathe. Still crying, I took Sam's tiny hand in mine, soaking it with my tears.

A doctor then informed us that Sam had suffered severe brain damage from the accident and suffered a minor stroke during his surgery. He explained that since the car had struck him in the head, crushing his skull, there was now fluid build-up in and around the brain. The pediatric neurologist, Dr. Cole, had inserted a temporary shunt into his skull to help drain the swelling. It was an hour-by-hour thing. The doctor said that every hour he survived was a good sign.

Sam was completely dependent on these machines. He couldn't even breathe on his own. Every few minutes, another nurse or doctor came to our bedside to check on my son. Any wrong decision could lead to disastrous results. I held his hand, praying that he was not feeling any pain, because I could not bear it if he was. I had to believe that he was resting peacefully, blissfully unaware of what was going on.

It was getting late, and the hospital found us a place to sleep on the second floor. Nathaniel kept telling me to go downstairs to "our room" and rest. How could I rest while my little boy was laying there, more dead than alive? However, by two in the morning, I did finally take Nathaniel's advice. I would be of no use to my son if I fell to pieces. I needed to get some food and rest, after which I would have more strength to help my son the following day.

I fell asleep crying like a baby. When I awoke, I had no idea where I was. I had forgotten everything that had transpired the day before. When it hit me that I was in the hospital and that my son was three floors up fighting for his life, I just crumbled and began sobbing all over again. I cried so many tears over the next few months, I could have filled an ocean and then some.

By the time I returned to the ICU later that morning, I was a different person. I had made a conscious decision to do everything in my power to make sure that Sam would be okay. I would reach out to the most competent doctors and surgeons. I would be at his side 24/7, and make sure no mistakes would be made. My little boy would get the best care possible.

Sam's condition fluctuated from stable to critical so frequently, it was difficult to remain calm. There was a machine that gauged brain pressure due to swelling. If the numbers rose dangerously high, they would have to decide how to alleviate some of the pressure. He constantly had fever, and that needed to be watched closely. I insisted on an update from the nurses every fifteen minutes, and my eyes were glued to the numbers on all his machines. I watched to make sure they were not getting too high or too low. The doctor warned me that we had to prepare ourselves mentally for the possibility that he might not pull through. I told the doctor that there was no way Sam would not pull through. I refused to even contemplate the thought that he would die. It wasn't an option.

I monitored his temperature, and noted when it went up even slightly. The nurses were not concerned with these small temperature elevations, but I wasn't taking any chances. I would stuff ice into those latex-free hospital gloves and place them all over his little body, turning them over every few seconds so he wouldn't get too cold. If the brain pressure gauge elevated an iota, I would literally scream for the doctor.

Every day that Sam lived was a good day as far as I was concerned. And every day that passed was one step closer to his recovery. We'd made it through the first twenty-four hours. Yet every time I thought we were "safe", the doctor would burst my bubble by reminding me that Sam's condition was still very critical. What kept us sane was the outpouring of phone calls and emails from people who'd heard the news and wanted to help. I didn't even know half of these people. They'd never met my Sam, but they cared.

I began emailing everyone I knew, and begged them to say prayers and do good deeds in the merit of my son's recovery. The internet gave me the forum through which I reached out to thousands of people, worldwide.

As the days went on, Sam began looking worse. Fluid was building up in his head, causing it to swell. I noticed that there were no marks on his arms, legs, or chest-not a bruise or scratch. The car rammed into his head, so his body was the right size, but his head was four times its regular size.

There were two doctors on the pediatric ICU floor, and their personalities could not have been more different. The first doctor who walked up to my son's bed was Dr. Rubin. He was a kind man who always took his time checking that everything was as it should be. He would never rush me, patiently answering every single one of my questions. He was an extremely optimistic person. Every day, he would look at my Sam and tell me, "This kid is a fighter. I just know he is going to pull through this." This gave me hope and some desperately needed peace of mind.

Dr. Rubin handed me a Make-A-Wish application for Sam. This wonderful organization grants wishes to children who are very sick. I wanted to cry. I wasn't sure my son would ever be well enough to be granted a wish. But Dr. Rubin insisted. So I spent an hour the following day filling out the application, praying to God that Sam would recover enough to receive his special wish.

By the second week, we were introduced to the second physician on the floor. I asked her all the same questions, "Is my son going to be okay? How much longer until we can take him out of his induced coma? Will he ever be the same?" She always looked worried, and responded to all my concerns with the same sad look on her face.

"Is my son going to be okay?"

"We just don't know the answer to that."

"Will my son ever be able to walk again?"

"We'll just have to see."

She had no words of encouragement. She was a real Debbie

Downer! Maybe she was afraid to get my hopes up. But what advantage was there to being sad and pessimistic about the situation, even if it was the truth? Perhaps a better truth and reality can be created and developed by our thoughts!

Dr. Rubin decided that Sam was going to pull through. That was his hope, and that is what I assumed would occur. The other doctor saw my son and decided the statistical chances of his being okay were almost zero. I know about statistics, Little Doctor! I am all too aware of statistics. They mean nothing to me.

During this difficult time, my parents were there for us every minute of every day. We would take shifts. Nathaniel would cover the morning shift, I would be there all afternoon, and my mother or father would cover the night shift. My devoted parents were the ones sleeping on those notoriously uncomfortable chairs at his bedside. I don't think I could have survived this period of time without their endless amount of love and support. I also knew that no one would take better care of my little boy when I was not present. I knew he was in good hands.

I remember the first weekend after the accident. Nathaniel stayed with Sam in the hospital, while my father and I were at home watching my two daughters. My father helped me get the girls to sleep, and then we just sat at the kitchen table in silence. We had no appetite, so the thirty casseroles we received from well-meaning friends and neighbors sat untouched (sorry, everyone).

Although my parents were there for us, my mother was having a very difficult time dealing with this new reality of ours. She would threaten to kill herself (from grief) every day, and we worried she was dead serious, pardon the pun. She needed to be watched at all times, and we sought psychological counseling, where she was given medication to help her survive this initial period. My mother was on slow-mo at this point in time. She was really drugged up good.

I didn't have that luxury. I needed to be fully alert and vigilant of everything that was going on, if I was to make sure that my son would be okay. I had to watch everything the nurses and doctors were doing.

I pleaded with everyone I knew to say prayers for Sam. I knew God was listening. Maybe He was waiting for more of our collective prayers. My mission was clear. I needed to reach as many people as I could. Prayers were said for him in every country around the world. I asked people to do an extra kind deed every day. Maybe, in my own little way, I could help bring a bit of peace into this crazy world. Maybe this whole event was designed to remind people to pray for others, and improve as individuals. Maybe it happened in order to bring people closer together. I had no idea, but I did believe that if people prayed and did good things in the merit of my son's full and complete recovery, then God would listen. I received hundreds of emails from people whom I'd never met, telling me the good deeds they'd added to their everyday lives. Tens of thousands of people all over the world were praying for my son, and I knew deep in my heart that all these prayers would reach God.

My son was only two years old, and he was changing the world around him in so many good ways.

Yet, the hours of each day at the hospital went by verrryyy slowly. I would watch the clock above Sam's head, and sometimes, it even seemed to be ticking backwards. Each day was an eternity of suffering and fear. One day, his vitals seemed to improve. By the next day, they'd declined.

Each day, I read and talked to Sam. I would hold his hand and tell him all kinds of stories. I kissed his hands and cheeks a thousand times daily. I kissed his little fingers, not knowing if I would ever see them move again. I kissed his lips, not knowing if he would ever call for me or smile again.

The time had come for the doctors to surgically remove the shunt which had been draining all the excess fluid around Sam's brain. There was still a tremendous amount of fluid build-up. However, the doctors were concerned about infection and serious complications if the shunt was left in place for too long.

A feeding tube was surgically inserted into Sam's stomach. He could not eat, but his body needed nourishment. This alone added more tubes and machines to my little boy's bedside. His arms and legs had to be tied to the bed so that he wouldn't move involuntarily, further injuring himself. The therapist would come in once a day to try to move his body so that his poor little muscles wouldn't atrophy. The hospital ordered customized "boots" for him so that his feet would remain straight. It just didn't end.

For one month, Sam's status remained stable, but unchanged.

It happened on a Monday morning, I was resting in one of the hospital rooms, when I heard a knock on the door. I didn't want to answer it. I was exhausted and really not in the mood to deal with anyone or anything at the time. Dr. Rubin persisted.

"Mrs. Harot, get up, your son is asking for his mommy."

I jumped out of bed and opened the door. "Are you serious? Are you sure?" I sprinted up the stairs and ran down the hallway.

What I saw next was probably the most beautiful sight I had ever seen. Sam was awake! His eyes were fully open and he was smiling. I ran over to him and said, "My darling boy, Mommy missed you so much."

He didn't say a word. He didn't move, but he did keep smiling at me. My boy woke up! I wanted to shout it from the rooftops. Look everyone, my boy woke up! Look what God did! Sam is going to get through this! And now, we all would.

The doctors and nurses all rushed to his bedside, both excited and shocked to see the boy who had almost no statistical chance of waking up had opened his eyes. Many of them just looked at him in disbelief. My son was back!

For weeks, I'd hoped and prayed that he would awaken. That was the first miracle I requested from God. After Sam smiled at me, I said, "I thank you for this, but I need my boy to have a full recovery." I went so far as to ask God to make Sam better than he was before the dreadful accident. After all, this was God I was talking to. He split the sea, and before that, He created the whole world. He could do whatever He wanted. All He had to do was snap His fingers.

Now I would begin to grill the doctors about how bad the brain damage was. Would he ever be able to walk, talk or sit up straight?

The answers were unchanging. When I asked Dr. Rubin, he told me, "This kid is gonna walk out of here one day, happy and healthy." When I asked Dr. Debbie Downer, she said, "He has suffered severe brain damage to his frontal lobe. This affects everything in the body, so it is hard to say if he will ever be able to do anything again. We need to wait and see what happens."

Just to let you know, that was the last time I ever spoke to Ms. Downer. I wanted nothing to do with her. When it was her week on call, I just ignored her and kept all my questions in my head, waiting for Dr. Rubin to come and answer them.

One day, my mother and I were at Sam's bedside, with my mom singing all of Sam's favorite songs. Sam smiled for the second time, and let out a little giggle. It was the sweetest sound I had ever heard. His head was still as big as a watermelon, and his face was distorted due to the multiple skull fractures, but at that moment he was the cutest thing I had even seen.

I loved that smile. He started becoming real again. It was as if he'd returned from the other side to the land of the living, and I was there to witness the whole miracle firsthand.

Slowly, he learned to move his arms and legs again. Sometimes, his limbs would convulse uncontrollably. The doctors explained that it is common for brain-injury patients. But it wasn't common for me! Each time it happened, it frightened me more than before. I prayed that this was temporary, and that his body would soon relax and not jerk unpredictably.

We began sitting him up in his bed, propped by a heap of pillows. He did not have the ability to hold himself in that position, but if we held him there, we could feel his exertion, trying to steady himself on his own.

His recovery was now progressing at a miraculous pace.

Every day he was able to do something new. Every day, we were more and more encouraged by his progress. I felt God's presence in that hospital more than I had ever felt it before.

News of Sam's miraculous and continuous recovery spread and people started praying even harder. Everyone knew that his recovery was an absolute miracle, and it just made them want to pray more. I began speaking in schools, and telling the children about Sam and his ongoing miraculous recovery. People who'd never met him felt strangely attached to my boy. The kids would tell me all the kind deeds they were doing for Sam. It was a beautiful thing.

I would tell them,"Each and every one of you are part of this miracle! Each letter, each word, and each tear that you shed to God, adds another neuron which Sam will use to reach another goal". The kids I lectured were always amazed. I think it was the kids who really prayed the most. Sam was their modern day miracle.

Back in the hospital with Sam, I began to discuss the reality of Sam's brain injury with Dr. Rubin. Sam's frontal lobe was completely destroyed. There was absolutely nothing we could do to get it back. Damage to this lobe can cause problems in motor function, problem solving, memory, judgement, and impulse control. It is where our emotions and personality are stored.

However, the brain is unlike most organs in the body. When damage is done and the pathways in the brain are roadblocked, the brain can actually rewire itself so that new roads are paved, to allow the information to get to get to where it needs to go. In addition, different areas of the brain can, in a sense, learn to take over the functions that were lost.

The goal of rehabilitation therapy is to stimulate the brain to create these new circuits or roadways. In order to do that, the brain has to be challenged constantly.

Even though Sam's frontal lobe was completely destroyed, I fully believed that through proper therapy we had a chance of his regaining back some, if not all, of what was lost due to the traumatic brain injury.

The most rapid recovery occurs within the first three to six months after the injury. The doctor advised me to work diligently with Sam once I got to the rehabilitation center, since the probability of Sam's recovery is greatly reduced after that six month time frame. I knew then that the next six months of my life would be dedicated to working with Sam, to gain back as much as we could.

It would be a marathon. There was not one minute to be wasted. I had six months to get my Sam back to a fully functioning, happy, healthy, two-year-old boy. Talk about pressure! But okay, it was good pressure. I had some power here. There was something I could do; there was a lot I could do.

There was not much rehabilitation given at the hospital, since their main concern was keeping him stable and preventing infection. I left that all up to them, but I began working on his skill development. I worked diligently to strengthen his muscles. Not only had he lost every function he'd once had during the first two years of his life, he'd been lying in a hospital bed for two months, unable to move. So his body was in serious need of a good work-out. I became his personal trainer from that moment on. One wondrous day, Sam sat up in his bed, all by himself! His perseverance, resilience, and endurance was quiet incredible!

He began eating real food. Okay, baby food, but it was better than his getting all the nutrition from that awful feeding tube. He had to relearn how to swallow and how to chew. I was not kidding when I said that he had to learn everything from scratch. He was like a newborn baby, but instead of taking years for him to learn things, his brain and body worked in fast-forward. He was recovering at an astonishingly rapid pace, which was amazing to see. He made new strides every single day.

The hospital provided him with a special stroller, and we were finally able to safely get him out of bed. Sam and I began doing our laps around the nurses' station and back. It was a step-or many steps-in the right direction. Every day, I would lift him out of his bed and try to get him to bear the weight of his body on his legs. He really didn't like this very much, but I was a tough general. I knew I couldn't be deterred by whether he liked or disliked something. I couldn't be soft-hearted when he was tired. We had a deadline here, and I was driven to get him to that finish line.

I began placing Sam into a standing position. He held onto the side of the bed, while I supported him by his waist. We did this once an hour, but for a few seconds longer each time. I would encourage him by telling him how proud I was. When he smiled, I knew he understood. Slowly, I began to let go a little more each day, until finally Sam was standing. All by himself! It was a very exciting day; a huge milestone.

Sam began to talk, just a few words at first, but then more and more, even with his tracheostomy. I read him books and talked to him all day long. I downloaded excellent educational apps for him to watch when I was not present. I was bombarding his body and brain with so much information, but he was fine with it. He just became smarter and stronger, and that was extremely encouraging.

The time had finally come for our son to leave St. John's Hospital. Three months had passed, but it was the most miraculous three months I have ever lived through. Now we were heading to the rehabilitation facility. Just one more stop before heading home.

We had done a lot of research to find the best place for him. We finally chose The Children's Specialized Center, a branch of The Robert Wood Johnson Medical Hospital. The facility was known for having the best therapists, and in my mind, that was the key to getting Sam back and running, literally.

The place could be likened to a well-oiled machine. One therapist was better than the next. The day was always structured around his therapy. He would receive approximately five therapy sessions a day, each running forty-five minutes long. I followed him to every session. He had a speech therapist who would work on his swallowing and eating abilities, as well as language development. The physical and occupational therapists worked on strengthening his cognitive skills and upper and lower body strength. I thought **I** was a general, but compared to them, I was the candy man. They pushed, pushed, and pushed some more. I loved them for that.

After his therapy sessions were over, I would take him into the playroom, and we would begin our homework. Some of the time Sam was cooperative, and other times not so much, but I worked him hard regardless. I would find all kinds of incentives for him. I used stickers and lollipops. You name it, I used it. Why not? Sam was trying really hard, and he deserved it.

About a month into rehab, we began coaxing and cajoling Sam to take his first few steps. He was hesitant, but because he was such a brave little boy, he tried. At first, I would hold his hands like you would when teaching a baby how to walk. It was exactly the same thing.

One day, he actually did it. I went a few inches in front of him and said, "Come on, little guy, you can do it," and he did! He took his first steps, for the second time in his life, but this time, it was an absolute miracle. The radiant smile on his face showed he knew he had done something amazing. My son shocked the most trained and competent doctors in the rehabilitation world by taking his first steps that day.

We were progressing at a record pace. Normally, the kids at the center receive four hours of therapy per day. My Sam, however, received fifteen hours of therapy per day. I, his crazy and insistent mother, became his most relentless therapist. I worked continuously, with both his physical and neurological challenges. I was driven to reteach my son everything by our six month deadline. Each time he completed a puzzle, another group of neurons were created. We had to create thousands of new pathways in his brain. The more he worked, the more pathways he would create.

Sam was walking more and more each day. Admittedly, he had a funny gait, more like a wobble, but he managed to get around just fine.

The tracheal tube was still in his throat, which made it very difficult for him to talk. This frustrated him, because there was so much he wanted to say. Every morning, the nurses would clean out this tube, expelling the excess mucus that had accumulated from the day before. It was equivalent to a doctor sticking a 12 inch ruler down your throat every single day. He hated it, and I hated it even more. Every morning, the nurses would have to hold him down to suction the device. Sam would gag and choke and cry his little eyes out.

Those big, blue eyes would plead, "Why are you letting them do this to me, Mommy? Get them to stop!"

I couldn't take it. I would tell them to hurry and that it was enough, but they never listened. It would take them a good ten minutes a day until they finished this procedure. They were numb to his screams and cries. Hasn't my son gone through enough already? I thought miserably. Why are you doing this to him? Why can't you just leave him alone?

I had to hold myself back from crying with him. It was unbearable to watch. I wanted to punch the nurse on the side of her head each time he gagged. There would have definitely been some kind of lawsuit, but I couldn't care less. If I hit her in the head hard enough, she would definitely stop torturing my child.

During the second month of our stay, I was working with Sam in the playroom. He was having one of his daily coughing fits, but this time it seemed worse. He wasn't complaining or crying, he just looked different. Then I noticed his face, it was turning blue. Something was stuck in his tracheal tube and he was choking. It took the nurses close to fifteen minutes to dislodge whatever had been stuck. I stood there horrified, and crying my eyes out. My son couldn't even cry. He couldn't cry because he could barely breathe. He was suffering so, yet he never once complained.

He was such a happy and brave soul. When we took our daily walks through the halls, Sam, (or "Mayor of the Floor" as the nursing staff called him) would wave to everyone, flashing his fantastic smile. It was contagious. You just couldn't be in a bad mood after he smiled at you, or gave you a big warm hug. He just overflowed with love and goodness. Anyone lucky enough to be near him would be "magically dusted" with his light and love. He was a breath of fresh air and pure sunshine.

When living in a children's rehab center you see a lot of suffering. I met a mother from Iran, who had a two year old son, a happy and healthy toddler. Like most healthy children, he was very active and kept her hopping. It is quite humorous to see that no matter where you are in the world, kids are always kids. A toddler is a toddler. She was dressed very differently than I was. She would come to the rehab center every day, fully covered in black. I talked to her sad eyes daily. And she told me her story.

One day, while still in Iran, her son developed a fever, which landed him in the hospital. He ended up needing a minor surgical procedure. But there was a complication, and her son stopped breathing mid-surgery. The doctors resuscitated him, but his brain had been deprived of oxygen for too long, and damage had been done. When he awoke from his surgery, he was not the same child. He'd lost his ability to walk and talk.

Her child had entered the hospital with merely a fever, and had gone home with permanent brain-damage. So she'd brought her son to the United States in the hope that someone would be able to help. Here we were, two mothers from two vastly different cultures, yet as mothers, we were both helping our sons survive.

During our second month at the rehab center, Sam's schedule was working well. Nathaniel would watch Sam every morning from 8:00 a.m. until noon. After he left, I took over. I slept in a small apartment four blocks away which was designated for families of children who were patients at the center. Sam really didn't need us with him during all waking hours, but I didn't trust anyone else. I was hyper-vigilant about his care.

I remember one day, Nathaniel got stuck in traffic and told me he would be late. I rushed over to the center at about 9:30 a.m. to make sure that Sam was okay. I found him harnessed into his stroller, watching TV, and covered in food. I didn't even bother complaining to the nurses. They were so overworked and understaffed; it really wasn't their fault. I always say, no one is going to take care of your child like you or your family. I cleaned up my son, took him out of his harness, and shut the TV.

There were so many children in the rehab center whose parents couldn't be there all day because of work or other family commitments. This facility was supposedly one of the best rehabilitation centers in the country. These children were getting great therapy, but there are twenty-four hours in the day. What were these kids doing with the other nineteen-and-a-half hours? Okay, kids need sleep, so let's figure on ten hours of sleep per day, which still leaves nine-and-a-half free hours. This time was mostly spent in front of the TV, literally killing time which many of these kids really didn't have the "luxury" to do.

So by ten o'clock that morning, my son was clean, and in the therapy room with me. We would walk and talk, and play all kinds of fun games. Everything I did with him had a purpose. Every single second I spent with my son was precious, and needed to be utilized efficiently. If I wanted him to be a happy and productive adult one day, I had a lot of work ahead of me, and so did he.

Every day he learned something new, and every day he progressed. I asked the therapists why Sam was taken in the elevator instead of using the stairs while heading to the therapy room. I was told that he just wasn't ready to tackle the stairs. How were we going to know if he could achieve it if we didn't let him try? After enough pushing, the therapist said okay. Sam hated those stairs. The actual physical strength he needed to put forth to go up each step, and the amount of brain power he needed to get his feet to do what his head wanted them to, was extremely difficult for him. After four days of building up his endurance and coordination, he climbed up a whole flight of stairs! Yes, it took us over an hour and the therapist looked like she wanted to kill me, but Sam did it. He was drained after that, so I let him rest for a few minutes but only a few minutes. We still had lots to do.

After being with my son all day, I a found a volunteer from a special organization called Chai Lifeline to help me. I thought it beneficial for Sam to interact with other people as well. I knew this special volunteer would give Sam her undivided attention, and that Sam would enjoy the friendship. Often, she would bring him a toy or a game. That was his treat for the day. Yes, he had me playing with him all day, but to him that was work, and he was right. When the volunteers came, it was just fun play, which I knew he needed as well.

The volunteer program helped us throughout this difficult period. Chai Lifeline would bring us pizza once a week, and every night I knew there would be someone dropping off a warm dinner for Nathaniel and I, so that we had one less thing to worry about.

My team of "prayer-sayers" would ask me how Sam was doing, and I would repeat the same mantra, "Keep praying to God. Whatever you're doing is working!"

It was fascinating for me to see how many people felt so close to my boy. Strangers, people whom I'd never met in my life, each with their own stories and struggles would come up to me in malls and food stores and ask if they could give me a hug.

During our stay at the center, I decided that I wanted Sam to appreciate everything that everyone was doing for him. It was time to somehow pay it forward. I tried to figure out what a two-year-old could do to help other unfortunate patients at the rehab center. All kids, no matter where they live and who they are, love two things: candy and toys. I headed to our local toy and candy shops to begin my shopping.

After accumulating three white garbage bags full of toys and candy, I brought them to the center. I asked Sam to help me distribute the toys to the children on the floor. His initial response at seeing the garbage bag filled with toys was, "I want it all!"

My kid was an angel, yes, but he was a two year old angel after all! I tried to explain to him that he could pick one toy for himself, and that we'd be giving the rest to the other children to make them happy. My generous angel was okay with that, so we were ready.

I put one bag on the back of Sam's hospital stroller. The other two we carried by hand. We visited every single room, and by the time we were done, we had given out most of our toys. Our mission was a true success. Sam had made some very sick children smile that day.

After six weeks in rehab, Sam's body had stabilized enough for the doctors to give us permission to head downstairs on our own. That was a very special treat. The second floor was nice, but come on, how could you compare it to the hustle and bustle of the lobby? It was heartwarming to watch my son's face the first time we went down. It was as if I had taken him to a different planet. He watched everyone coming and going with such fascination. This was a new world for him, a world that he had been missing for the last few months.

On another such day, we headed out on our adventure to the lobby. There was a gentleman standing in front of a cardboard kid's size firetruck. What is the obsession with toddlers and firetrucks? Sam was ecstatic. The man had boxes and boxes of chocolates behind the paper truck. It looked like heaven to a chocoholic like myself. I asked the man how much a Snickers Bar cost. He told me that the chocolate was all free. He owned a chocolate store, and this was his way of giving something to the kids. I was so thankful to this man who thought of the sick children. I realized at that time how much goodness there is in the world. I asked Sam what kind of chocolate bar he wanted, and he kept changing his mind.

He was torn between a Snickers bar, a bag of M&Ms, and a Kit Kat.

The gentleman smiled and said, "How about you take all three?"

Sam let out a shriek of delight. We then sat there in the lobby for an hour, just watching people go by, as we savored our chocolate. I think only thirty percent of it made it into his mouth. The rest ended up all over his face, in his hair (yes, in his hair), and all over his shirt. He was "choc-lified" and gloriously happy. My heart melted.

THE GREAT OUTDOORS

THE DAY HAD FINALLY ARRIVED when I was permitted to take my son outside. Remember that Sam had not been outside for five full months. He had no idea "an outside" even existed. He was like a baby, starting everything from scratch. I don't think he had any memories from before the accident. His whole world had been hospital rooms and lobbies.

The weather was a bit chilly, but the sun was shining brightly. I knew the facility had their own little playground and I would watch it from the window, but I never knew if Sam would be strong enough to enjoy it. Now, only two months after being in rehab, we were ready to try. He used to love swings, but now I was not quite sure. He was a totally new little boy. His likes and dislikes were totally different from before the accident. There were so many foods and activities that he avoided before that he now enjoyed. The brain is just such a complex organ.

The first thing he noticed was a little rocking horse on springs. He began his funny little toddler-run, and flew over to the little horse. I placed him carefully on the back and showed him how to rock. He rocked back and forth, smiling from ear to ear. Next stop was the swing. It was a big industrial-sized swing with numerous belts and buckles. The therapist made me close each and every one. It must have taken me five full minutes buckling him in tight, but he didn't seem to mind. He was just enraptured by everything around him. This was a fantasy world for him.

I slowly began to push the swing.

It felt as if time had slowed down for those few minutes and everything, every sound-every color-every feeling more vivid and more filled with life than I have ever felt before. The sun was a bright, beautiful ball of warm, sweet light. The tree branches were swaying in the wind as if performing a delicate dance in honor of my son's special day. Birds flew above Sam's head and sang a song of peace and happiness. It felt as if I was on a movie set from one of those Disney animated features where the blue bird would fly onto my shoulder and sing me his sweet song. Ok, there was no blue bird but I tell you that if one did land on my shoulder at that moment I would not have been the least surprised. For those ten minutes my world was in perfect harmony and mother nature jollied in to be apart of the celebration.

I watched my son fly high into the sky. I didn't see the swing or belt buckles. I just saw these amazing majestic blue eyes that had the power to melt my heart. He smiled from ear to ear and he let out a screech of such pure and innocent delight that it made me want to cry. I watched as his little toddler legs began kicking in excitement each time the swing would head high. I watched his beautiful golden blond curls fly high into the sky grabbing the sunlight to make them look almost magical. This little boy of mine asks for so little and is happy with even less. When given the most basic childhood activity, a day outside to swing, he took it as the best present he could have ever received. I knew then that this son of mine had a soul of grand proportions. This soul I thought will do something very special in this world one day. It was the perfect day in every possible way.

My Sam was just an old soul, and still is. He has this unique and unusual wisdom that a typical two year old hasn't had the time to acquire. He was like an amicable ninety year-old man "wrapped" in a two year old body, and the combination made him so genuinely lovable that anyone who met him just wanted to eat him up.

In our culture and in our day and age, the older someone gets, the less important they become to society. So we strive to retain our youthfulness forever. Don't get me wrong. I have no problem with wanting to look and feel young. I think eating right and exercising are important, and how I wish I had the body I had when I was twenty.

But I think a lot of us are missing the point. Yes, it is good to be young, but it is good to be old as well. First of all, what is the alternative? We are all going to get old, whether we like it or not. It is far better than not getting old, if you know what I mean.

There is something very special that comes with age, namely, the knowledge earned from a life filled with experiences. Sit down with your grandparents and great-grandparents (if you are lucky enough to have them), and actually talk to them. Most have been there and done that. The old adage "there is nothing new under the sun" is quite insightful. There is nothing in this world that is all that different from the way it was a thousand years before. The physical exterior of things might seem different. We now drive around in cars and use our smart phones for practically everything. They didn't have these items eons ago, but they did have love, hate, war, peace, anger, and jealousy.

Trust me, whatever someone is going through today, there has been someone who has experienced something almost identical hundreds of years ago. Try to explain this to a teenager, and they will probably slam the door in your face, and only realize how right you are when they become older and wiser.

I once read an article written by an older man. He was complaining about the younger generation, and how they don't treat the elderly with the respect and esteem that is due them. The article stated "this generation is all about ME. The young believe they are eternally in the right. This is the problem with the youth of our generation!"

The author of this article was none other than Aristotle. I was shocked and amazed. Aristotle lived over a thousand years ago. You mean, there were crazy teenagers then too? Is that possible?

Years go by, seasons change, world powers thrive and then they die. Yet the essence of the world that God created will always stay the same. Human nature remains unchanged, as does almost everything else in this world.

One fine day, the center informed us that our insurance would no longer cover our stay. The therapists and doctors concurred that it was safe for us to bring Sam home. For me, however, this was another battle.

No way! Here, he was getting almost five hours of therapy a day. Once we got home, my insurance would cover only two forty-five minute therapy sessions a week! That just would not do. Sam was still so far from his goal. There was so much that he was still unable to do. They seemed to have forgotten that we had a deadline to meet. He had proven to be a success as far as they were concerned, and they were basically done. I begged and pleaded with everyone, from the receptionist all the way up the corporate ladder, but with no success.

Before discharge, Sam was taken by ambulance back to St. John's hospital to surgically remove his feeding tube. The doctors wanted to keep his tracheal tube in place for another two months, since he was scheduled to undergo two major surgeries for which it would be needed. I'd assumed when I finally took my boy home, the horrible plastic tube emanating from the big gaping hole in his throat would be gone. But I would never want to compromise my child's safety, so unfortunately the tracheal tube came home with us.

HOMECOMING

I T WAS MID-SPRING, AND THE sun was shining brightly. I remember putting Sam in his little car seat, telling him we were going home. He was excited. For him, this was an adventure.

Sam was always excited. You could tell him that we were going to pick weeds in the desert, and he would be excited. He was just so happy with life. It didn't take much to make this kid smile. I knew that I had a lot to learn from my son.

It was a very special day. He had no idea what "home" meant. He had lived at 5 Tremont Rd. all his life, but had no recollection of any of it. There was a great big sign on the door saying, "Welcome home, Sam!" and it was signed by forty neighborhood kids who loved and missed Sam very much. As we entered the house, my daughters started arguing over who was going to pick him up first. Everyone wanted a piece of him, and he didn't mind at all. We let him walk around the house, carefully following right behind him so that he shouldn't fall.

Within two weeks of his being home, I decided to send Sam back to his playgroup. I was not sure if he was ready, but there was only one way to find out. The teacher was delighted and surprised.

Even though everyone knew about the ongoing miracles in Sam's recovery, many doubted he would ever come home, due to the severity of his injuries. To see this kid back on his feet in less than six month's time was beyond what even the top doctors could have ever imagined.

Even though Sam was home, he was still far from being "fixed". His face was still distorted, and he could scarcely see out of his left eye. He would need multiple and extensive micro-surgeries to fix some of the injuries that he had sustained. The first of his surgeries was a two-part, full-day operation. The first half of the surgery was performed by Dr. Rubin. This surgery would seal the perforation in the membrane surrounding Sam's brain. It was a complicated surgery with many risks that I tried not to think about.

After four hours, we were told that Dr. Rubin had finished his segment of the surgery. Now it was up to the pediatric eye surgeon to complete the rest. We found a top-notch doctor to work on the orbital bone around his eye. It had to be repaired, and it was a very intricate and delicate procedure. By the end of the day, we were all emotionally drained.

At last, both doctors emerged, reporting that they were happy with the results. Sam remained in the hospital for a few days, and they were difficult days. His whole head was bandaged up like a mummy. His face was black and blue and severely swollen. Again, he didn't look like my son. My poor son felt miserable. I didn't know what to do for him.

For the first twenty-four hours, he was not allowed to move. Do you know how hard that is for a two year old? Ask a typical two year old to lie down in a bed and not move for a full day. It just isn't happening. So the doctors had to literally tie him down to the bed, which made him even crazier. He was so unhappy, and watching it made me feel sick to my stomach. I also knew that this was not going to be the last of his surgeries. He was scheduled to have at least two more major surgeries to repair the skull fractures, as well as repairing his left eye socket.

By the time he was transferred from the ICU to the pediatric floor, he was mobile again. Together, we would walk around the halls, dragging his mini IV pole behind him. Of course, Sam wore a pediatric size hospital gown, wide open in the back for all to see. I remember watching him do his thing walking up and down the hall with his little bottom just hanging out. It was beyond adorable. He was such a trooper. His head fully bandaged, and attached to a truck load of machines (which of course beeped all day long), he still managed to smile.

Sam eventually completed three more surgeries. The accident had fractured many bones, which had dislodged the eyeball as well. Since his eyes were not fully aligned anymore, his right eye would see a different image than his left. An adult with this problem would likely have to wear a patch on one eye. It would be maddening to consistently see two different images.

Sam lost eighty percent of the sight in his left eye, so we were instructed to begin patching the right eye in order to strengthen the left. Slowly his vision began to come back. We would patch his right eye all day for many years.

When we took the patch off, his brain did something miraculous. Instead of seeing two different images, due to the misalignment, his brain now automatically shut off the vision of one eye. If you would cover his left eye, his brain would allow only the right eye to see, and if you covered the right, he would see solely out of the left. Because his brain was still so trainable, it adapted in this way, enabling him to only see one image instead of two. Amazing!

Since Sam had to walk around all day with a patch on one eye, we decided to buy him the coolest patches we could find. We opted for the dinosaur/pirate package, since Sam was absolutely obsessed with both. I didn't know how we were going to keep this patch on. It was not comfortable and, remember, he was only two years old. I was sure he pull it off every day. Sam never once tried to pull the patch off, nor did he complain. It was as though he understood it had to be done, and there were no questions asked. He accepted it graciously, just like everything else in his life.

One day we were walking down the street, when a bunch of kids yelled out, "Look at that boy! He has a funny Band-Aid on his eye!" Sam just smiled, and called back to them, "This isn't a Band-Aid, this is my special patch!" He was absolutely adorable.

The third surgery was finally completed, and Sam was successfully able to see out of both his eyes. He would still need to be patched for four hours a day, until he was nine years age. I asked the doctor if Sam would be able to drive one day, and live a normal life. He said, "He might not qualify for the Air Force, but this kid is going to see just fine."

FOUR IN THE FREEZER

I STILL HAD THE DREAM of having a large family. People would say, "Another kid? Are you out of your mind?" But I yearned for the chance to have one last sweet baby to nurture and love.

Preceding the past surrogate pregnancy, my husband and I still had unused frozen embryos. Four little guys in the freezer were waiting to be thawed out and nurtured in a nice, warm place. My four little guys! Incredibly, our gestational carrier was ready for her second round. She began with the tests, medication, shots and hormones for several months. Two of my little guys were taken from the freezer and, after months of working with our gestational carrier, the day finally came to introduce them in utero, where they could grow and be happy.

We received the call ten days post embryo transfer, Unsuccessful. Neither embryo had survived. We had one more chance. We followed protocol. We had the best doctors, the best medical care for our surrogate carrier, and our second set of little freezer buddies looked great after a long thawing. I kept thinking about these freezing-cold cuties saying to themselves, "They finally took us out! It is about time. We were freezing in here."

I was sure it was going to work this time. The doctor said the embryos looked perfect, and our gestational carrier's body was ready to receive the second and final embryo implant. Her uterus was lined to perfection, and all the other fertility mumbo-jumbo sounded good and ready to go.

The ten-day mark was on a Friday, and I remember checking my cell phone to make sure the ringer was on, so I wouldn't miss the call.

After what seemed like forever, the doctor's office called with results.

"I am so sorry, Mrs. Harot" the nurse told me. "The blood tests have come back negative. She is not pregnant."

I think the doctor felt terrible, and conveniently delegated this phone call to his nurse.

The finality of me never having another child was hard for me to accept. I didn't know how to feel. I'd asked God for something, and He'd answered me. The answer was no. I was sad for the loss of what could have been. It was a difficult pill to swallow, but I knew that I was beyond grateful with everything else God had given me in life.

THE DECEIT

Not long after Sam's accident, our thriving clothing business went into bankruptcy. Nathaniel and I were struggling to stay afloat. We had returned to work full-time, as soon as Sam was somewhat stable.

Why had our sales plummeted by over fifty-percent?

During subsequent months, our sales dropped even further, close to eighty-percent! Something just didn't add up. A rival business had opened up around the same time. But I was sure our competition was not the reason behind such a huge lapse in sales.

We went to work every day and tried to come up with different strategies on how to market ourselves better. We tried everything. Sales, promotions, advertising campaigns. You name it, we did it. I even rented a bunny costume one Sunday, and stood on the corner of 57th St. and Main Ave wagging my bushy, white tail and handing out fliers to every passerby!

By the way, the whole passing-out-fliers-thing was beyond humiliating. Only the cover of a costume saved my self-esteem. People just pass you by, purposely avoiding eye contact with you, as if they'd turn to stone if they looked! Am I giving out sticks of dynamite? I guess I too am one of the people who look away when the flier-giver-outers approach me. They can be a little annoying. The most persistent ones usually get me to take the flier. I stick it in my handbag. Then I find it months later, obscured by scribbled notes, and a big wad of ABC gum stuck to the back.

Frankly, I believed our managers and workers were stealing. I mentioned this to Nathaniel numerous times, but he always disagreed. Years before this, I'd begged Nathaniel to fire all the managers and start anew. I sensed they were taking advantage and stealing from us. I didn't trust them at all, and wished that he would listen to me and take charge. But it never happened. Nathaniel preferred to pretend that all was well. I had no choice but to listen to him and work with our dishonest managers for years and years.

However, nothing could have prepared me for the full extent of deceit that was going on behind our backs. Or for the news we were soon to find out.

One of our employees entered the office, crying and looking very scared. She began to tell us a story that sounded so outrageous, I hoped it wasn't true. She revealed to us that while we were in the hospital trying to save our son's life, the managers from our different business locations joined forces and began stealing large amounts of money. They knew we were "busy" in the hospital and rehab centers. These unscrupulous individuals, who'd worked for us for over ten years, for whom we'd given big bonuses, took everything we had. It was the ultimate betrayal. This was not accidental or unintentional. This was a malicious act of pure evil. They knew our whole story, and took that opportunity to rob us blind. There are just no words to describe the anger I felt.

As soon as we found out, we called the police and filed a report. We never received a penny back, and the workers got away scot-free. We were told we did not have enough evidence, and legal fees were not something we could tackle right now.

Nathaniel fired everyone on the spot.

I was furious, not only with the workers but with Nathaniel as well. I had been begging him for years to fire these managers, because I was sure they were stealing. I had told him they were all in it together. I'd asked him to put in cameras. Inexplicably, he did nothing. He watched as our business (which we'd spent ten years sweating over) was being taken from us. Like a diamond left unguarded, our business was left in the hands of crooks.

Much as I'd suspected some dishonesty, never in my wildest dreams did I ever think our managers would have the audacity to steal everything. They were clever. I have to give them that. They overlooked nothing.

Believe it or not, the managers called Nathaniel the day after they were fired, and actually asked to be paid the money we owed them for their last week of work. Are you kidding me? Are you serious? I couldn't believe the gall these people had!

I knew that I would never again see the money they stole

from us. The only thing I could do at this point was tell them how I felt. I asked the two managers to come to my house at six p.m. if they still wanted their paychecks. Before they arrived, I had decided exactly what I was going to say. I hid a small camera in the corner of the room hoping to get them to admit to the crime they had committed. I would send it to our lawyer.

The doorbell rang. When I opened the door I saw my two managers, with an unfamiliar man by their side. He must have been 350 pounds and over 6 feet tall.

They thought they could intimidate me with this guy? Are you kidding me? (They obviously never read this book!)

They had no idea whom they were dealing with. I looked straight into their eyes, and with an eerily calm voice I told them "When you go to sleep at night, I want the image of my son plastered on to your brain. I promise that you will pay for the damage you have inflicted on my family. If not through us, God will see to it."

As they left, I swore to them that if they ever came near my family again, I would make them truly sorry. I had no idea how I would make good on that promise, but I did know that my Mother Hen gene would never allow someone to do something like this to us, ever again. Years and years of hard work, using every penny we had to invest into our business-only to have it stolen by thieves, masquerading as good, ordinary people.

This financial loss affected us on every level. We couldn't pay our basic bills, and we lost our health coverage due to non-payment. For the next five years, we had no source of regular income. I waited and waited for Nathaniel to step up to the plate and figure out a way, any way, to provide for our family financially. He tried to open a few smaller businesses along the way, but each one failed more miserably than the last.

I realized that I was going to have to try something on my own. Since my original goal in life was to make people happy, I would work towards that goal. That's when my brother and I came up with the idea of a candy, chocolate gifts, and frozen yogurt shop. I couldn't imagine a place that could make people happier. I mean, come on. Kids in an ice cream/candy store? A dream!

I will never forget the conversation I had with my brother. He said to me "Emma, you've tasted so much bitterness in life. You deserve something sweet and happy from now on". Now that is a brother.

I told him that I still kind of owed him for loaning me some of his precious bone marrow. After this, I would really owe him big time. My kind, caring, and generous brother helped me invest in this new business. I was ready to start all over again.

I decided to call my store the Twisted Gourmet Chocolate Company. I was heady with excitement for this new chapter of my life to begin. At the same time, I was also very scared. I knew nothing about creating frozen yogurt or selling candy! I knew business, and I knew how to sell a product, but Fro-yo and candy were never my thing.

I spent over a year designing and creating the perfect happy place where people could come and put their stress away (albeit for just a half hour) and enjoy my bright, fun, and colorful store. Customers find themselves in a life-size Candy Land board game. I am proud of my little shop, and I believe it is making a small difference in people's lives.

But it is ten times more work than I could have ever imagined. I figured, how hard could it be? It's all self-serve? Right? Wrong! It is a lot of work. I run the cash register, create my own flavors, clean and sanitize the machinery, make smoothies, bake muffins, work the espresso bar, and clean the squished cookie dough and stepped-on rainbow sprinkles off the floor. I do the ordering, delivering, banking, and advertising. I manage the social media aspect, and recently added customized gourmet chocolate gift arrangements (as per my clients' specifications) as well. I am doing my part, and I hope and pray that God will bless my efforts with success.

In January of 2017 we were granted a wish from the Make-A-Wish foundation. Sam loved everything ocean-related. He loved sharks, whales, and any sea creature you could possibly imagine. His dream was to swim with the dolphins and whales. Well, the whale part would be tough, but swimming with the dolphins could be arranged. The organization arranged for our family to take a trip to a family resort in the Caribbean. There, he received a private one hour swim session with six dolphins and three trainers. I have never seen my child smile as wide as he smiled that day. He took me in his arms and whispered in my ear "Mommy, this is the best day ever! I am so happy." There are just no words to describe how I felt at that moment. I closed my eyes, and thought about Sam in his ICU hospital bed. Dr. Rubin was right. Sam would receive his wish.

I never forgot the man with the firetruck who had graciously given out the free chocolate in the rehab center lobby many years back. As soon as my candy business got off the ground, Sam and I began volunteering at various children's charities. We made hundreds of candy bags and Sam smiled as he handed each one to another sick child. He said he was going to say a little prayer for all the children. That is my boy. He has a heart of gold and a soul that is rare to find.

A Team Divided

NATHANIEL AND I HAD BEEN deeply in love for almost twenty years. I took it for granted that it would always be this way. The trials and tribulations we endured together made our love stronger. However, at some point along the way, our love began to dwindle, overpowered by building resentment and anger. It didn't happen after the first, second, or even tenth challenge we went through together. But the last few tests that hit us began to erode at my assumption that we would always be in love.

It began with our vehement disagreements on how to deal with Alex, when she began getting into serious trouble. This horrible phase of hers definitely marred our relationship-how could it not? Nathaniel believed that no matter what Alex did, we should "let it go". I was adamant that we had to set strict limits for her. The truth may have been somewhere in the middle, but Nathaniel insisted it had to be his way. We were on opposite teams, and I felt it. I felt betrayed by the one I'd once loved the most. The second assault on our relationship was the car accident, and the "nail in the coffin" was the demise of our financial security.

Until now, we'd never had to deal with major financial stressors. Yes, we had our tests in life, but money had never been one of them. We went from owning a thriving business and living a life of absolute financial comfort, to counting pennies for the weekly grocery order.

Additionally, Sam needs specialized schooling. That, my friends, doesn't come cheap. Even with the best insurance, there are hundreds of thousands of dollars that need to be spent.

Nathaniel and I argued over money whenever bills came,

which was basically every day of every month. It just got harder and harder. When you have financial security, it is hard to comprehend how hard life can be without it. You need money for just about everything!

Money may not "make you happy" but I can tell you from having experienced both ends of the spectrum that anyone who tells you "money is not important" is either stupid or filthy rich! Money does give you choices in life. Each time I thought I had somewhat of a grip on our bills, they would pile up all over again. I could not allow the bank to foreclose on our home! Sometimes I didn't know what to do, or where to turn. Living is an expensive proposition!

COUNT YOUR BLESSINGS

W HEN SPRING OF 2017 ROLLED around, I believed that with new buds blooming on the trees in my yard, I too would be revived, and continue to fight life's battles with renewed strength and courage.

Sam started first grade in the fall. He could not contain his excitement. I beamed with joy, watching this happy child wait for his bus to arrive. On this spectacular morning, Sam picked a large red flower from our garden, and squished it into his lunch bag. He said it was a present for his teacher. My heart was glowing with pride. My boy was back, and he was awaiting the school bus like every other healthy child. I tried to hold onto this feeling of pure bliss.

Nathaniel began a small business that is helping to pay some bills. I am working my hardest at Twisted Gourmet to make it successful.

Marriage is tough, because life is tough. But Nathaniel and I are fighters, true-blue. We are committed to doing whatever it takes to make our relationship work. I am focusing on the qualities that made me fall in love with him in the first place. We are trying to be kind to each other again, and our earnest efforts are definitely paying off. Don't get me wrong. Our marriage is a work in progress, just like everything else in life. It will always have its ups and its downs. However, we are now working together as a team to raise our beautiful children. We are both letting go of the anger and hurt, and have promised each other never to let go again. We need to hold on tight, to get through this journey we call life. Love is blossoming again.

I heard this great allegory. Life is like a beautiful tapestry. We humans only see the underside of the cloth, with loose strings and a ganglion of knots. It is certainly not pretty.

Eventually, however, we get to view the front. All those loose strings and knots that were such a mess on the other side, have actually created a beautiful, perfect picture.

Our tapestry is going to be a beautiful work of art!

Dear Reader,

Thank you for taking the time to read my story. If you are going through one of life's tests, no matter what it is, then I hope this infuses you with the courage to face tomorrow.

You are never alone.

I know life seems unfair. I know all too well. But keep telling yourself that, in the end, it will be good. It is not a matter of if, but when. I had to believe in that basic principle to get through everything I've dealt with, and still deal with, to this very day. **God has the power to do anything.** There is no reason why He should deny you happiness. If you are not there yet, just know you are still on your journey, but you will achieve true happiness. Just have faith and hope. Always hope.

Our individualized journeys will never be easy, but they are meant to bring strengths we didn't know we had. I was meant to live a zig-zag life, as I call it. My car started on the highway like everyone else's, and then I hit a continuous stretch of road blocks. I was forced to detour off the highway, and take many backroads.

In the end, the ones who have suffered experience life to the fullest. For we experience the beauty and majesty of the high mountains, as well as the pain and anguish of the deep valleys.

When we get to the end of our journey, we will appreciate every happy moment we had, and every nook and cranny of that final destination. Nothing will be taken for granted. How can one truly understand the concept of authentic joy, if one has never felt despair? How can one fully appreciate anything in life, if, at some point, he has not lived without it?

So, to the people who are living a zig-zag life with me, congratulations! We are the ones who are chugging up that mountain, like The Little Engine That Could. Keep going, no matter what hits you from seemingly out of nowhere. You do yours, and God will do the rest. He will not let you down.

As for me, I truly hope that this is my last tough chapter. May the rest of my life be ordinary and simple.

It is nightfall, and my children are worn out from an energetic day of play and laughter. I lie down next to Sam and put my head to his chest. He looks so peaceful. He takes my hand in his, and falls right to sleep. I lie there with him for hours. I never thought that I could love something or someone as much as I love my family.

I lean in and give my miracle boy a kiss. The house is quiet, the kids are tucked warmly in their beds. My eyes shed a tear, as I look up to God and pray for health, happiness and peace. I truly believe that's what He wants for us all.

THE END

Printed in the United States
By Bookmasters